The Walk II

Choice & Consequences

ISBN: 978-1-257-96789-6

Acknowledgements

I give all praise and glory to my Lord and Savior Jesus Christ. He leads and guides me in the way in which I should go even when that is not the way I would always choose. He knows what is best for me. I only have to agree with Him by choosing what He has already chosen. I want to thank the love of my life Gwen for loving and supporting me during the good times and bad. I want to thank and acknowledge my brothers, Larry Eubanks Sr., Nate Escamilla, Calvin Pitts, Rory Bernard, Sean Slavin, and Robert Allen. Your wisdom, insight, and friendship helped me during a very difficult time in my life. Thank you for being there for me.

Preface

Before you make a choice you are the master of it. Once you choose you become its slave. The life that you are living right now is the sum total of all the choices you made in the past. Deuteronomy 30:19 says, "I call heaven and earth to witness against you today, that I have set before you life and death, the blessing and the curse. So choose life in order that you may live, you and your descendants." Many people think that they can randomly make choices and that they are the only ones affected by them. Nothing could be further from the truth. The choices we make affect everyone in our lives, those with us in the present and also those to come in the future. We bless or curse future generations by the choices we make today. Every choice you make is the first step on the road toward somewhere. As a society we need to develop the ability to look beyond the instant gratification of our flesh and decide if the destination that our choice is leading us is the place we want to be. The same thought process that we use when taking a trip is the same that we should use when making life choices. When most people plan a trip they already have a destination in mind before they start their journey. Some of the things that they consider before deciding on a destination are the cost, how much time the journey will take, and what attractions or points of interest are at their destination. If they are traveling by car they will Map Quest their trip by inputting their starting point and destination to get the route, mileage, and amount of time the trip should take. A lot of forethought and planning usually goes into planning a trip. It is unfortunate that most people do not think about the destination that their choices will take them. The poems written in this book are all based on real life situations. Some people believe that experience is the best teacher, but I believe that someone else's experience is the best teacher. As you read these poems do so with the awareness that someone else has experienced the consequences as a result of the choices that they made. You receive the benefit of seeing where their choices led them. Most people believe that when you die you do not take anything with you. I believe that there is something that you take with you and it is the decision to accept or reject the gift of salvation only found in Jesus Christ. This is the most important choice you will make in your life because the result of this choice has eternal consequences.

Barrett D. Taylor

Contents

Poor Little Runaway

Poor little runaway, why are you so afraid?
Your former life is behind you
All things have become new

You were once a slave in your former master's house
He abused, used and turned you out
You were content to eat the scraps from your master's hand
You were a home born slave you had no desire to leave his land
One night some ex-slaves snuck onto your master's land
They told you about Jesus and how to escape from your master's hand
Their words were like fire and created a desire within you
You answered Jesus call and a new heart He gave you
You packed up that very night to begin your spiritual quest
You became so discouraged and confused at your very first test

You left all your old friends
You left your master's home
You entered a new land
Now you feel so all alone
Everything seems so different
Everything seems so new
You have to think for yourself
Many times you don't know what to do

Times are very hard
Nothing seems to be working right
You start thinking about your former life
When the master fed you from his very hand
You say this new life is too hard; I'm going back to the master's land
You return to your old master
He's been waiting for you
All the time you've been gone he's been thinking about you

You run back to him thinking everything will be the same
He beats you in front of the other slaves
He locks you up with chains
He puts you to hard labor
He gives you food that's unfit to eat
You left the burdens of freedom
You lost wayward sheep
Now your latter condition is worse than the life you had before
He afflicts you seven times greater; he gives you seven times more chores

Journey across the Sea

You joined the crew of the Carpenter
For a journey across the sea
You left the land of your forefathers
For a place of peace and liberty
In the midst of the journey you encountered a storm
And your ship was tossed to and fro
The waves rose so high that you thought you would die
As the Carpenter rested within
As the lightning flashed and the thunder crashed
You lost sight of your Savior and Lord
As the storm threatened to sink your tiny ship
You forgot that your Shepherd was aboard
Just as you thought that the end had come
You cried out, "Lord, do you not care?"
"I trusted you to see me through
To a land without any cares"
Then the Carpenter awakes
And with a mighty quake
He stands up and rebukes the storm
Then He turns to you, and he sees right through
To the very depths of your soul
He says, "Oh you of little faith, do not fear,
But only trust in Me!"
"My word is true and I'll surely do,
Everything that I promised to you"
"If you should suffer in this life for My name
Great will be your reward"

Tear Down Your Father's Altars

....Why is the land ruined, laid waste like a desert, so that no one passes through? And the Lord said, "Because they have forsaken My law which I set before them, and have not obeyed My voice nor walked according to it, but have walked after the stubbornness of their heart and after the Baals, as their fathers taught them. Jeremiah 9:12-14

It's time to tear down your father's altar
It's time to go another way
Now is not the time to falter
For this is a brand new day

It's time to stop worshipping the idols
That your parents bowed down too
Your life will remain in idle
If rebellion is found in you

It's time to tear down all the images
That your fathers conformed too
It's time to receive wisdom and knowledge
Put all falsehood behind you

It's time to break the chains of tradition
That worshipped man instead of God
It's time to walk in another direction
Though the people think you're odd

It's time to commit your life to the Lord -
Even though it may seem hard
It's time to read what's in the bible –
And accept it in your heart
It's time to stop doing business as usual –
Barely surviving from day to day
It's time to take God at His word –

And live your life the Bible way

Don't look back, Don't look back
You're a new creature in Christ
Don't look back, Don't look back
Live the overcoming life
Don't look back, Don't look back
You're no longer a slave to sin
Don't look back, Don't look back
Obey the Lord and you will win

Repair the Walls

"You have not gone up into the breaches nor did you build the wall around the house of Israel to stand in the battle on the day of the Lord." Ezekiel 13:5

You just gained a mighty victory
You just repulsed the attack of the enemy
You almost tripped but you didn't fall
In the heat of the battle the enemy breached your wall
He came attacking in one direction but ran away in seven
The Lord your God sent angelic help to assist you from heaven
You fought the good fight and now it's time to celebrate
You say, "Now it's time to party, repairing the walls can wait!"
You tell your testimony to encourage others
You sit around and swap war stories with your brothers
And all this time the breaches are in the walls
If you don't repair them they will lead to your downfall
The enemy gathers all his forces to spring a surprise attack
He will catch you off guard because your hand was slack
In comes the enemy and he catches you unaware
When your head was in the clouds and you thought you had no cares
Now your city lies desolate, the walls are all broken down
Instead of a smile on your face you walk around with a frown
One defeat does not mean that it's the end
If you trust in the Lord you already have the win
Disobedience caused your downfall; obedience will raise you back up
Sometimes you don't learn that lesson until you drink from that bitter cup

Your Choices Affect Others Besides You

And so to speak, through Abraham even Levi; who received tithes, paid tithes, for he was still in the loins of his father when Melchizedek met him. Hebrews 7:9-10

For as through the one man's disobedience the many were made sinners, even so through the obedience of the One the many will be made righteous. Romans 5:19

Noah made a choice and saved his family
Moses made a choice and set the captives free
Jesus made a choice to redeem humanity
Your choices affect others besides you

Adam made a choice to disobey God
As a result humanity has had a rough road to trod
Through the one all became sinners and life became very hard
Your choices affect others besides you

Joseph's brothers sold him into slavery
For many years in remained in captivity
He chose to forgive his brothers and saved his family
Your choices affect others beside you

David chose to take a census and count every man
He forgot that it was God who helped him to stand
As a result of his sin a plague covered the land
Your choices affect others besides you

Solomon was the wisest man on the earth
God favored him since the time of his birth
In his latter years he worshipped idols and caused the land to be cursed
Your choices affect others besides you

Paul endured much suffering as a soldier for Jesus Christ
Nothing could deter him from doing what was right
Through his writings people are still learning to live the Christian life
Your choices affect others besides you

Your friends are doing drugs and you take a second look
It started out as fun but now you're hooked
Your family is in trouble because all you owned the dope man took
Your choices affect others besides you

You chose to finish high school and college too
When you graduated a six-figure income was waiting for you
Your children live a better life because to your dream you remained true
Your choices affect others besides you

At school you were the life of the party
Your parents tried to warn you but you wanted to be free
Now you're unwed with four children living in poverty
Your choices affect others besides you

You made a mistake early in life
You had a baby with a woman who was not your wife
But you manned up and remained in your child's life
Your choices affect others besides you

You wanted to be a player and sleep all around
You left a trail of broken homes and babies all over town
At your funeral no one showed up, only your parents came around
Your choices affect others besides you

You had an unplanned pregnancy and you started to stress
You wanted to tell your parents but you was scared to confess

You had an abortion and now you're mentally a mess
Your choices affect others besides you

You chose to keep your baby instead of aborting him
You refused to bow down to the pressure exerted by them
Your son pastors a church and many lives have been changed through him
Your choices affect others besides you

You lost your job and you were very sad
When you couldn't find another one you became very mad
You went back to school, learned a trade, and now your family is glad
Your choices affect others besides you

The economy dropped and you fell on hard times
To supplement your income you chose a life of crime
You haven't seen your family in years because you're doing hard time
Your choices affect others besides you

Your neighbor's home is full of strife
They get abused by their son almost every night
Through your prayer and intervention God has set things right
Your choices affect others besides you

You chose to accept the Lord Jesus Christ
He delivered you from a sinful, unproductive life
Everywhere you travel you carry His light
Your choices affect others besides you

The choices you make affect others besides you
The consequences of your choices impact those connected to you
When you make bad choices you cause your loved ones pain

But when you are successful their joy cannot be contained
Every decision you make affects your unborn seed
Submit to the Holy Spirit and ignore your flesh's greed
Future generations are depending on you
To do the things that you ought to do

I call heaven and earth to witness against you today, that I have set before you life and death the blessing and the curse, so CHOOSE LIFE in order that you may live, you and your descendants. Deuteronomy 30:19

Nourish the Root, Produce Good Fruit

Children are a gift from the Lord, a gift that He entrusts
Our job is to discern the talents within; recognition of their gift is a must
We must remove our preconceived notions of how everything should look
Prayerfully intercede for your children and follow the instructions in the Book
Raise up a child in the way he should go and he won't depart from it
The enemy comes to kill, steal, and destroy its time you get used to it
Many times we try to fulfill our dreams though the life of our child
Unfulfilled dreams accomplished through our children keeps us satisfied for a while
But God placed within each of us a seed that will produce fruit
Our job is to nourish our children's mind so that the seed will take root
Frustration comes when we don't discern what God placed inside our child
We try to lead them in a way God didn't intend causing them to react so wild
The behavior that seems so inappropriate to you is appropriate in the proper place
Swimmers don't run in marathons; make sure your child is in the right race
Wisdom is hidden deep within a man, and a wise man draws it out
The place of agreement is the place of power, there's no need to scream or shout
Trying to solve a problem without a plan only leads to frustration
Sit with wise counselors and draw up battle plans to get your child to their proper station
Rebellion comes when there is frustration because both sides cannot agree

Nourish the root, produce good fruit, and then your child will walk in liberty
A violent struggle takes place as a caterpillar tries to break out a cocoon
Your child's gift is too big for his environment you must make some changes soon
The seed of the righteous shall be delivered, this we know to be true
God gives wisdom to all who asks and He will see you through
Continue speaking words of life over your children for this is what you were called to do
Nourish the root to produce good fruit and one day your child will thank you

Worry is Worship

Who you bow down to is a choice you must make
Blessings or cursing, which one will you partake?
Man was created to worship and this he will do
Don't let your circumstances choose who you'll submit too
All of God's promises are written in His book
Take more than a casual glance, take a long hard look
What you find there will give you strength in the day of adversity
His promises give you peace as you face an enemy called worry
Trouble always comes to steal the Word from your heart
If your foundation isn't strong from His way you'll soon depart
Worry works hand in hand with a spirit called fear
If you see one of them the other is always near
Worship is submission to the Lord of your life
Don't depart from your First Love like some adulterous wife
Praise belongs to the Lord no matter what you go through
This trial isn't strange, trouble isn't unique to you
The words in your mouth reveal what's in your heart
The Lord finished the work now it's time to do your part
Your eyes and your ears are the doorways to your soul
What you choose to feed on will make you timid or bold
A carnal man can't please God and he always puts Him to the test
He looks at his world and worries instead of entering His Rest
We must worship the Lord in Spirit and in Truth
We do external worship but our mind is on a commute
Thinking about things that open us up to fear
We do a self examination to determine why He isn't near:

"I paid my tithes and my offerings too"
"His words says he'll never leave nor forsake you"
"When others are in trouble I always intercede"
"Now that I'm in the thick of it He hasn't met my needs"
"I'm always there to comfort a grieving friend"
"But no one is there for me when it looks like the end"
"I always forgive others when they offend me"

"So why am I a prisoner chained in captivity?"

STOP! IN THE NAME OF JESUS!
"THESE THOUGHTS MUST LEAVE ME RIGHT NOW!"
"WORRY IS NOT MY LORD AND I REFUSE TO BOW!"

I will no longer entertain these demonic thoughts
It's time to start doing the things I've been taught
You're in a church where the Word is preached
If you practice what you've learned many people you'll reach
The Word comes then trouble comes, the pattern is clear
This is not some strange thing so don't submit to fear
There's no defeat unless you agree
In Christ you've already overcome the enemy
Don't bow down to worry, lift your voice and confess
Jesus is Lord and in His Presence I will rest

Judge Yourself

Nothing is impossible to those who believe
Have faith in the Father; there's nothing you can't achieve
Don't let doubts blind you, but let His love find you
No matter what obstacles you face continue in the race
Is anything too difficult for the Lord?

It's time for you to unsheathe your sword
The Word of God is His will for You
To qualify for the promise there are things you must do
It's the doer, not the hearer only who will be blessed
Mental assent without action will keep you in that mess
From the abundance of the heart, the mouth speaks
If your words don't agree with God's then its wisdom you should seek

If you continue to walk in defeat although your environment has changed
Then it's time to judge yourself; you can't afford to remain the same
Insanity is doing the same things expecting a different result
It's time to stop being children and start being adults
Love will sometimes offend those closest to you
Transparency precedes intimacy; this is what you must do
Speaking the truth in love is the only way
The results manifest tomorrow, although you feel the pain today

Wrong Beliefs Will Bring You Grief

Honesty is the best policy there's no getting around that
If truth isn't your chief pursuit you'll never locate where you're at
To get to where you're going here is where you have to start
You must be honest enough to look back, and see where you started to depart
Away from the Lord and His plan for your life
How can you know peace when all you've ever known is strife?
When you believe someone else's lie it is an unseen snare and trap
Once you locate the truth you can be redeemed from that
But if the deception comes from within it's harder to discern
Others try to teach you but you're unwilling to learn
Anything that you believe that contradicts what God says about you
Are seeds sowed by the enemy to hinder your breakthrough
There's a saying that says eat the meat and put aside the bone
But if there's poison mixed in with the meal you should just leave it alone
Once the poison is in the food it is spread throughout
When it gets inside the body it starts killing from the inside out
The words that you speak produce death or life
They produce homes that are peaceful or those full of strife
We place so much emphasis on the things that we see
When it's the unseen things that should have our priority
We're so careful about who we sow our money too
But we expose our minds to whoever comes through
Our minds are shaped by the things we are taught
We just open up to anyone, that's why the deceiver isn't caught
We haven't yet made the connection between what we do and what we hear
We don't deal with the problem until ungodly behavior starts to appear
Who's influencing your thinking? Where's the ultimate source?
The things you're taught and believe is what sets your life course

Renewal of the mind is so vital you see
You cannot claim God's promises until you and He agree
No one is born a racist, this behavior is taught
Flesh and blood is not our enemy, that's not where the battle must be fought
By the time someone starts walking in the things that they've learned
It's been imbedded in them so deeply that it's hard for them to turn
My life is the manifestation of what I've been taught all my life
If you say something contrary to what I believe you're just trying to create strife
In their mind they are right and everyone else is off key
"This is the way things always were and it's the way it'll always be
So man fights against man and it just creates division and hate
Some look at skin color before they choose their mate
Body of Christ it's time to stop playing games
No matter what your skin color we all go by the same name
Christian is who we are, sons of the Father of Lights!
Is Christ divided? We all know that racism isn't right!
Don't you know you were bought with a price and your life is not your own?
It's time to take up the Father's thoughts and leave the old thinking alone
Our vision is too limited, we can't get pass what we see
The tent that I now occupy is not a permanent habitation for me
The things that are eternal are the things you can't see
From an eternal viewpoint I'm identified by the Spirit which indwells me
There are only two races of people; Satan's and God's very own
Wherever your daddy lives is where you'll call home
You're no longer a slave; you have eyes but cannot see
The devil isn't your friend; he's your eternal enemy
Our attitudes about others are the things taught in our homes
Renew your mind with the Word of God and leave that old thinking alone

Every time you go back to the nest, those old words you start to hear
Confronting your family's bigotry is your biggest fear
We must make the decision that the buck stops with me
I won't allow those spirits to manifest on my branch of the family tree
I am a new creation in Christ Jesus and the Master has made me free
The things I used to believe no longer have no dominion over me
I will always love, intercede, and be a witness to my family
No longer will I be held in bondage because of what they think about me
Be strong and courageous in the Lord Jesus Christ
If you cover your light others will keep wandering in the night

Broken Focus

It's not good to stay at home
In times of trouble you shouldn't be alone
Don't meditate on what you fear
But quiet yourself so you can hear
Now is not the time to speculate
This is not a season to vegetate
You have physical symptoms but you're not caught
Practice the Word that you've been taught
Spiritual Warfare isn't hocus pocus
All defeat comes from broken focus
First you must remove the weeds
Think righteous thoughts, do righteous deeds
When people and things come with a negative report
With the Word of God you must retort
Make up your mind regardless of how you feel
That your times are in His hand and His Word is real
In the midst of your trial Satan sends people to you
They are unwitting servants who don't have a clue
The fact of the matter is they might be Christians too
And don't realize they've been sent to harass you
If a person doesn't bring with them the Word of the Lord
In a time of trial their company you simply can't afford
Whatever breaks your focus has mastered you
How can you walk in Light if darkness surrounds you?
Your mind is the place where the battle will be fought
It's time to put into the practice the things you've been taught
Don't meditate on your problems or on defeat
It's time to move on from the milk to the meat
When negative thoughts comes throughout the day
Come against the thoughts and the demon that sent them your way
Satan wants to break your focus, don't make this easy to do
Deception is what he'll use to turn you own power against you
Why do you think the devil has paid so much attention to you?

Could it be that he sees what God wants to do in and through you?
The devil's not omnipotent, he doesn't have unlimited power
He only directs his attacks against threats to his kingdom, this is a critical hour
For the joy set before Him Jesus endured the cross
Stay focused and you won't experience loss
Stop focusing on your problems and open your eyes
Meditate on the Word and let the Holy Spirit be your Guide
Have you forgotten who you are and who you belong too?
Have you forgotten the source of your strength and the promises He made to you?
You are a child of God; He hasn't given you a spirit of fear
You're seated in heavenly places with Christ; His Word makes this very clear
For the spirit of heaviness put on the garment of praise
The speed in which the devil will flee will have you simply amazed
When you offer the sacrifice of praise God will occupy your home
As long as you do this you will never be alone
Take your eyes off your problems and keep them on the Lord Jesus Christ
As long as you do this you'll live an overcoming life

It's Time to Grow Up

We spend so much time interceding for those
Whose present situation is something they chose
Doing the same things expecting different results
Acting like children instead of adults
Their world is falling apart but they are too stiff-necked to hear
Each day it's more of the same, living in a constant state of fear
In a multitude of counselors is wisdom, pride comes before the fall
Words of wisdom are near you, but you can't hear the call
You're confused and frightened so you seek others advice
You receive godly counsel but you refuse to sacrifice
The devil can only attack you where he has a legal right to be
As long as you walk in the flesh you'll never be free
Your dilemma is not related to what you see but what you do
And you will die in the wilderness unless a change occurs in you
Your world is falling apart around you and now is not the time to play
It's time to reconnect to God it's time to fast, praise and pray
Your world is a reflection of the life inside of you
If you change the way you think and you will change the things you do
Your world is falling apart around you and now's the time to fight
Resist those fleshly impulses, obey the Lord and walk in His Light
All that you're going through is subject to change
But it won't until you do, you cannot remain the same
God is trying to talk to you but you turned to Him a deaf ear
Your world is falling apart around you will you still refuse to hear?
Your life is the harvest of the all seeds that you have sown
You're eating the fruit of your choices now that those plants are fully grown
God never meant for you to live in poverty, confusion, and lack
If the devil has no place where can he attack?
Make a decision today to follow the Word at any price
Trust in the Lord Jesus, He has the power to change your life

He Must Increase

The Word without the Spirit is like a car without gas, a gun without bullets, or a television without electricity. You have structure, you have something you can perceive, you have something that looks good, but without a source of energy or the wrong source of energy it cannot accomplish its purpose. The reason so many Christians are ineffective is that they expend most of their energies in unproductive labors instead of being conformed into the image of Jesus Christ. We so readily excuse any thoughts or attitudes that fail to conform to the likeness and teachings of Jesus. We justify unforgiveness and withhold our prayers from the people who bring the most pain into our lives, (the very ones who need our prayers the most). We are so unwilling to allow someone to take advantage of us in the natural so that we can gain a victory in the spirit.

While we were still in the midst of our sin
Jesus died on a cross to provide the way in
Love motivated Him to submit to this task
He submitted His will to the Father and did all that He asked
As He is in this world so are we to be
Submitting our wills to the Father so that others can be free
He has given us every weapon to accomplish this job
But we haven't been very effective and to us this seems very odd
We fast and pray and read the Word
We are like children who hear but haven't heard
We go to church every Sunday and we meet in small groups
We expend much energy in our labors but haven't produced much fruit
We look for something to do to give us a sense of accomplishment
But at the end of the day not much has been done and our energy is spent
Jesus said, "Put My yoke upon you for the burden is light"

If your thinking is wrong how can you ever hope to do right?
As a man thinketh in his heart so is he
How can you help others escape if you are not free?
Any thoughts, ideas, or attitudes not submitted to Jesus Christ
Means that you are walking in darkness that appears to be light
When your life is not submitted to Jesus and you engage the enemy
How can you hope to ever gain the victory?
You must allow Jesus to be Lord of your entire life
He must increase, but you must decrease to live an overcoming life

Don't Hide, Abide!

You passed the test
You entered His Rest
The land is now at peace
In your soul you feel relief
But if you're not careful you'll soon feel grieve
Because your enemy won't readily admit defeat
The struggle was long but you have the victory
Your foot is on the neck of the enemy
The land is at peace and your soul is refreshed
You kick up your heels to take a little rest
But your enemy will not stay away
He only looks for a more opportune day
He hides in the shadows to hit your blindside
He sends small temptations to get you to compromise
He wants to move you from faith to doubt
He designs temptations to pull you out
When you totally trusted God you defeated the enemy
Submission to God is the place of immunity
Immunity from all the enemy's attacks
When you start to doubt God then your armor cracks
When you were small in your own eyes you trusted Him
Now that you have a few victories you think you don't need Him
You start to make decisions on your own
You separate from God and now you're all alone
You try to do His Will in the strength of your flesh
Now you're weary and tired because you're no longer in His Rest
When you're tired and vulnerable the enemy strikes
He hits you without warning like a thief in the night
Now your mind is filled with many cares
You feel so defeated you can't even work up a prayer
All you previously gained you feel you've lost
It's time to make another trip to the cross
There's no remission of sins without confession
If you hide your sin you can't move on to your next lesson

Darkness is where the enemy reigns
Confess your sins to God, keep it simple and plain
The sin that you excuse, overlook, or hide
Is the very place where the enemy resides
How can you have confidence when you kneel down to pray?
When you have unconfessed sin in your life everyday
The Bible says confess your sins one to another
To get back in right standing with your Older Brother
If you want to live a victorious life
Confess your sins and walk in the Light

Don't Give Up Your Confidence

And without becoming weak in faith he contemplated his own body, now as good as dead since he was about a hundred years old, and the deadness of Sarah's womb; yet, with respect to the promise of God, he did not waver in unbelief, but grew strong in faith, giving glory to God, and being fully assured that what He had promised, He was able also to perform. Romans 4:19-21

Christianity is not denying the problems that you face
It's denying that those problems can pull you out of the race
The devil is out there doing his job, let's start doing ours too
There's an outlaw in the land and he must be arrested by you
It doesn't matter what your circumstances are if God made a promise to you
Don't concentrate on what you see but know that what God says He will do
Stand on His Word no matter how many enemies you may face
His Word says where sin abounds He makes available much more grace
God's Word shall accomplish whatever He sent it out to do
The game isn't over no matter how things may look or feel to you
Nothing is too hard for God; all things are possible to those who believe
Place all your trust in God and many things you will achieve
The Bible is full of promises that God made especially for you
You must stand on those promises until they manifest to you
If we ask anything according to His will we know that He hears
By faith and patience you'll inherit the promise even if it takes several years
Don't be so concerned about the here and now but how it all will end
You can endure anything that you face if you know in the end that you win

There are some promises that in your lifetime you will not see come to pass
Future generations will be blessed because you didn’t run out of gas
Give glory to God in the midst of your trial and He will always appear
Worry and doubt will flee at His Presence, perfect love casts out fear
Don't be intimidated by the obstacles or the giants you will eventually face
Pace yourself and with patience and endurance you will finish the race

Remain in the Camp

And their children whom He raised up in their place, Joshua circumcised; for they were uncircumcised, because they had not circumcised them along the way. Now it came about when they had finished circumcising all the nation that <u>they remained in their places in the camp until they were healed.</u> Joshua 5:7-8

There's a war going on inside your mind
Hidden beneath the surface great treasure you'll find
You are born again and your spirit is renewed
If your mind is unchanged by the enemy it'll be used
The enemy operates out of a fortress of thoughts
What you do is a result of what you've been taught
As a man thinketh so shall he be
Until you think new thoughts you'll never be free
You can cast out the devil but if you leave him a place
He will just return later to get you out of the race
Renewal of the mind is a spiritual transfusion
If you think the wrong thoughts you'll come to the wrong conclusions
You must win the battle that you fight all alone
Before you engage the enemy away from home
Remove the beam from your eye before you start surgery on me
How can you free others if you're not walking in victory?
Don't excuse the sin that so easily besets you
If you don't acknowledge your weakness how can you breakthrough?
Fear is an enemy, start to see it as that
When fear comes upon you realize you're under attack
The presence of fear should indicate you can't do things alone
Those who acknowledge this fact demonstrate that they've grown
Many people want to war against the devil and his host
Some out of concern for others, some so they can boast
How can you help others if you aren't free?

How can you engage the enemy if you're in captivity?
Israel was circumcised before the attack on Jordan could start
There are some things that must happen before you depart
If you're dealing with issues like shame and fear
Before you engage the enemy there's some things you must hear
Remain in the camp until you are healed
Confess your sins to the Lord, don't keep them concealed
If you engage the enemy in a weakened condition
You probably won't be able to complete your mission
Stop looking at others and all that they do
Just trust in the Lord and He will reveal all to you
You can only give what you have received
Look at your true condition stop being deceived
We are just messengers, administrators of His grace
He gives you a package to deliver to a place
As you personally know the Lord you can minister to others
Deception is a tool of the enemy, stop hiding from your brothers
If you're walking around thinking the Lord has forsaken you
You won't be very effective in the thing you attempt to do
You want to go out and minister to wayward souls
You want to proclaim His word confident and bold
You want to raid the enemy's camp and set the captives free
You want to lead others to the Lord so they can be free
You want to witness on your job and administer His grace
You want to get others off the road to destruction and into the race
The Lord wants to use you in all these things
But if you aren't healed you'll be tormented by demonic beings
If I am a teacher and I am not free
How can I show you the way to liberty?
If I am a pastor who's fleecing the sheep
How can I demonstrate how to protect, hold & keep?
If I am a evangelist who sins at night and preach during the day
My life is not a confession of the words that I say
If I am a prophet and can't discern the voices I hear
Sometimes I minister life, sometimes I minister fear

If I am a apostle who leading the people to myself
I'm building my own empire and putting the Lord on the shelf
If I am a Christian who's not walking in the Way
People listen to what I do and not what I say
As the Lord ministers to you He also ministers to your brothers
Remain in the camp until you are healed and you'll be a blessing to others

Why do You Feel So Sad?

When you're born again all things become new
All your sins are erased and you're no longer you
Your house is the same but the change is inside
The Holy Spirit lives in you to lead, teach and to guide

Why do you feel so sad?
Your eternity is decided so smile and be glad
You've been raised up with Christ above it all
Now go and reconcile the victims of the fall

When you're in His Presence His light shines inside
Exposing the darkness that still tries to hide
His Word refreshes like sweet morning dew
You reject all the lies as your mind is renewed

Why do you feel so sad?
Your eternity is decided so smile and be glad
You've been raised up with Christ above it all
Now go and reconcile the victims of the fall

A mystery is uncovered things you never knew
The person you've known all your life is no longer you
The Lord separates all the wheat from the tares
He removes those bad habits as you shed all your cares

Why do you feel so sad?
Your eternity is decided so smile and be glad
You've been raised up with Christ above it all
Now go and reconcile the victims of the fall

Your mind turns away from the temporal things
Your eyes look toward heaven and the gifts that He brings
When you can see clearly you can't be deceived
All that you've given up you no longer grieve

Why do you feel so sad?
Your eternity is decided so smile and be glad
You've been raised up with Christ above it all
Now go and reconcile the victims of the fall

Be Careful Who You Let On Your Boat

You're sailing along on peaceful seas
Happy and contented as you can be
When someone out of the will of God
Crosses your path and together you trod
When this person comes into your life
Peace leaves and in comes strife
The Bible teaches you to forgive others their faults
This is the game they play to keep you caught
Once you sailed on quiet seas with clear skies overhead
Now each day is stormy and filled with dread
Like Jonah, these people know they're bringing trouble into your life
They realize full well that they're the source of all that strife
So you work all the harder to keep things afloat
And this rebellious person won't voluntarily get off the boat
If you want to get your life back on track
It's time to confront this person and say, "Hit the road Jack!"
When you kick this person out of your life
Peace returns and out goes strife
As they sink into the sea awaiting them is God's fish
By the choices they made they are getting their wish
Each person who comes into your life brings either good or bad
Test the spirit before you commit so you won't be had
It's better to put that person through a series of tests
Than to at some later date try to untangle yourself from a mess
In a multitude of counselors you'll find safety
Don't trust your own instinct find out their history
People operate in patterns and if you dig what you may find
Is that this person has a string of broken homes and hearts they've left behind
Check their credentials before you allow them on your boat
Keep the trouble out of your life and you will always stay afloat

A Letter to Him / A Letter to Her

A Letter to Him

Once upon a time you were madly in love
You and your wife fit together like a hand to a glove
You looked into her eyes and said, "I do"
Other options are gone; it's just you two
You served her as only a man in love could do
Just her presence aroused love's passion in you
You only had eyes for her; you were blind to all others
Never in your wildest dreams could you see yourself with another
But hidden within, deep down in your soul
Lying beneath the surface was a gaping hole
Something unfulfilled in your life
Unknown even to your wife
A time bomb set to go off at the right time
That would cause you to commit a spiritual crime
Whatever you desire you start to draw near
If you arrest those thoughts you avoid many tears
The scent of lust rose from your body in waves
Seeking another like you who was just as depraved
Like a dog in heat to her scent you were attracted
You neglected your family because now you're distracted
You fell under the spell of a Jezebel
A tailor made temptation straight from the pit of hell
You disconnected from those who loved you and left your family
In your mind you were convinced that you were not happy
You left the wife of your youth
And attached yourself to a prostitute
Someone just as selfish as you
Who doesn't care what you put your loved ones through
You were a man of God fighting the Lord's battles
Interceding for the lost and rebuking demons like cattle
A man of the Word and a man of prayer
Your place is here; home is not there

You know full well the consequences of sin
How could you let the devil tempt you back in
You are now back under the devil's dominion
He has things scheduled for you too terrible to mention
Rouse yourself; wake up from this sin induced sleep
Return to your Shepherd you lost wayward sheep
It's time for you to regain your dignity
Submit to God and He'll break the bondage and set you free
You may not be able to patch up things with your wife
But if you confess and repent you can come back to the Lord Jesus Christ

A Letter to Her

I know that he hurt you the day he went away
Forsaking all the vows he made to you on your wedding day
You gave up everything for him, even your name
Now that he's gone you think things will never be the same
You wrestle with your thoughts; "Maybe this is all my fault?"
Reject that thinking it's just the devil on a mind assault
What's on the inside of a person will eventually manifest without
It was only a matter of time until the whore in him came out
I don't care if you were the perfect wife
You have no control over his inner life
A person can only be tempted by something he desires
Don't blame yourself because he was a lowdown dirty liar
Hold your head up high and refuse to accept the shame
You took his name but the Lord has for you a better name
You are His dear daughter, the apple of his eye
Stop tormenting yourself, stop asking yourself, why?
This will all work together for your good
If you go through this trial the way a good Christian should
Don't separate yourself from the Family of God
They will support and be there for you like a heavily armed squad

Where sin abounds God gives much more grace
He'll supply all that you need to finish the race
He may be gone but don't let him steal your life
Your future is sure if you continue to trust the Lord Jesus Christ

Brother to Brother

Brother, stop living a double life
Brother, stop mistreating your wife
You're out of His will and your home is full of strife
Brother you should stay home and pray
The streets are no place to play
It's time to change your ways
Or you will be sorry someday

Brother, remove the filth from your eyes
Respectability is nothing more than a disguise
Brother what you're doing is not wise
Brother I'm appealing to you
Stop doing the things that you do
I'll always be there for you
Repent and the Lord will make your heart like new

Brother, your heart has turned so cold
I'm your best friend and this you must be told
You no longer hide but practice iniquity so bold
Brother don't let the enemy in
Don't give in to the sin
Don't let the enemy win
On Jesus you can always depend

It's time for you to repent and reclaim your life
It's time to apologize and make things right with your wife
It's time to rededicate yourself to the Lord Jesus Christ
Brother, get on your knees and pray
Change comes no other way
Redemption can be yours today
Brother this is what I pray

Weak-Willed Men/Strong-Minded Women

All the woes on the Earth
Are here as a result of the Curse
The Curse began at the fall of man
Eve was deceived and Adam failed to stand
God told Adam what he needed to do
Adam listened to his wife and failed to follow through
Because he was disobedient to the Lord's command
God kicked them both out of the garden
Men! Now I speak these words to you
Are you doing all that the Lord requires of you?
Has God given you instructions on what to do?
And your wife says, "No!" And vetoes you?
You know in your heart the way in which you should go
When God said, "Move Out!" Your wife said, "No!"
When God said, "Give!" Your wife said, "Whoa!"
She wants to reap instead of sow
God tells you to stay in place
And she has you running all over the place
God gives you a good word in due season
She refuses to submit to it for no apparent reason
You tried to raise your children in the way they should go
And she undermined you and you didn't even know
When God tells you to lead your home
Sometimes you must go it alone
When God gives you a vision for your family
Sometimes you can't wait until she sees
Carnally minded people tend to follow their lusts
So any decisions they make you simply can't trust
It's time to break out of your lethargy
It's time to shrug off passivity
It's time for you to take the lead
It's time to stop following the deceived
It's time to risk all for the sake of Jesus Christ
It's time for you to finally confront your wife

Whatever relationship you consider as being most vital
Has become the object of your worship, it's become your idol
Jesus says, "Remain in Me and do not depart!"
"If you love Me I must have first place in your heart!"
If you compromise your convictions because you fear your wife
You are a weak-willed man living a miserable life
In public you appear to be the head
But at home your wife wears the pants instead
Ahab was once king of Israel
Under his leadership things did not go well
Ahab was king in title and name
But Jezebel his wife was really running the game
Ahab was the king, but Jezebel ran his life
He was a weak-willed man who constantly deferred to his wife
She practiced witchcraft, idolatry, and other evil acts
The Bible clearly documents all of these facts
Through the wiles of one woman the whole country became toast
She single-handedly caused the nation to abandon the Lord of Hosts
In public Ahab appeared to be very kingly
In private he was a child being led maternally
He had authority over the nation, but not in his own home
He allowed his wife to entice him to sin and he never atoned
Jezebel used his authority to accomplish her evil tasks
She made decisions of State and didn't even ask
Many times Ahab didn't even have a clue
He just let Jezebel do whatever she wanted to do
Men, find the courage to take a stand for Jesus Christ
Weak-willed men will never earn respect from their wives
If you don't want your family to fall
Stop being misled and follow God's call
Even if you have to stand alone, step up and be a man
Trust the Lord and He will give you all you need so you can
No one said it would be easy fulfilling your purpose in this life
Face your fears! Dry your tears! Follow the Lord Jesus Christ!

Stand Up and Be a Man

Then to Adam he said, "Because you have listened to the voice of your wife, and have eaten from the tree about which I commanded you, saying, 'You shall not eat from it;' Cursed is the ground because of you... Genesis 3:17

It's time to stand up and be the man God called you to be
It's time to get serious about your calling and shrug off passivity
It's time to get serious about your vocation and act responsibly
It's time to take a stand; it's time to be a man

It's time for you to become the leader in your home
Now's the time for war, it's time for Satan to be dethroned
It's time to submit to the Lord, you're not in this battle alone
It's time to take a stand; it's time to be a man

You received your marching orders from the Lord Jesus Christ
You've been mentored and discipled, you know wrong from right
You compromise and sear your soul when you stop walking in His Light
It's time to take a stand; it's time to be a man

Like Adam God gave specific instructions to you
And you clearly understand what He requires of you
Eve was deceived but Adam knew what he was supposed to do
It's time to take a stand; it's time to be a man

God told Adam, "Cursed is the ground because of you!"
If you cut off the head then the body is through
Smite the shepherd to scatter the flock is what Satan wants to do
It's time to take a stand; it's time to be a man

You give in to some demands because you truly love your wife
But Jesus said that He must be the first love in your life
If you get this wrong then you have already lost the fight

It's time to take a stand; it's time to be a man

Adam listened to his wife and disregarded God
They got thrown out of the garden and had a hard road to trod
The peace you gain through compromise is just a façade
It's time to take a stand; it's time to be a man

Stop listening to the voice of the enemy
He wants to lead your family into captivity
God's desire is that you walk in victory
It's time to take a stand; it's time to be a man

Workplace Affairs

You're having problems at home and no one to talk too
You feel so all alone; you don't know what to do
Your emotions are churning, you feel like you're gonna burst
Thinking about your problems just makes you feel worst
At work there's a woman who's been friendly to you
You tell her about your problems, you ask her what to do
She seems to understand all your hurt and your shame
She speaks encouraging words that take away the pain

Workplace relationships grows into workplace affairs
People will split your home they don't even care
They are the hunters and you are the prey
If you don't watch your step sir, you could be alone someday

What you have done is allow a stranger in your home
If you don't be careful you could end up all alone
Intimacy develops by telling secrets to one another
Instead of talking to her you should talk to one of your brothers
What starts out as friendly talk turns to lunches in the park
You're an ignorant guppy being pursued by a shark

Workplace relationships grows into workplace affairs
People will split your home they don't even care
They are the hunters and you are the prey
If you don't watch your step sir, you could be alone someday

Lunches progress to friendly drinks after work
At home things are no better because your duties you have shirked
One drink too many and you've cheated on your wife
This is the beginning of living a double life
She puts pressure on you to spend more time
You tell your wife more lies about working overtime

Workplace relationships grows into workplace affairs
People will split your home they don't even care
They are the hunters and you are the prey
If you don't watch your step sir, you could be alone someday

Someone saw your car where it shouldn't be
They go and tell your wife now she's solved the mystery
Now you're sitting in Divorce Court splitting up your assets
You start to realize how much you lost now you're having regrets
The thrill is gone for the other woman because now she's your new wife
She keeps you on lock down you really miss your former life

Workplace relationships grows into workplace affairs
People will split your home they don't even care
They are the hunters and you are the prey
If you don't watch your step sir, you could be alone someday

The Wounds of a Friend

Have I therefore become your enemy by telling you the truth? Galatians 4:16

They hate him who reproves in the gate, and they abhor him who speaks with integrity.
Amos 5:15

But your iniquities have made a separation between you and your God, and your sins have hidden His face from you, so that He does not hear. Isaiah 59:2

It is not accident that I'm in your life
We were called together by the Lord Jesus Christ
Brothers in arms we are called to be
Protecting each other from the enemy
As I sow into your life, you sow into mine
If the enemy attacks you I respond in kind
When the enemy attacks me you have my back
Shoulder to shoulder we repel the enemy's attacks
I made a covenant with you before God and man
If you fall I promised to help you stand
You promised to be with me if I tripped and fell
Brothers united in combat, battling the hordes of hell
Brother, my feelings for you are no mystery
Just look back through our history
I've always told you the truth and I never lied
But you didn't deal truthfully with me and I don't understand why
I love you too much to keep these words within
I can't be a silent observer as you fall deeper into sin
I can't stand to the side and just pretend
I am compelled to speak the truth even if it offends
Better are the wounds of a friend than the caresses of an enemy
Deception leads to bondage but the truth sets you free
We gave each other permission to speak into each other's life

If we observed things that were not right
We promised to be truthful and honest without a fault
So when the enemy set his traps we wouldn't be caught
Why are you angry at me for telling you the truth?
Why don't you answer my calls and stand so aloof?
Why do you think I no longer care what happens to you?
Because I confronted you about some of the things that you do
He who loves correction will prosper in his way
Those who reject discipline will fall one day
Those with offended hearts separate from their friends
You must deal with the issues in your life if your heart is to mend
I love you with the love of Jesus Christ
I want to see you have a prosperous and productive life
Lies and deception are the weapons of the enemy
Satan can't cast out Satan, God's truth is the only remedy
If you look back over our history
My thoughts for you are no mystery
I was there for you in the beginning and I'll be there for you in the end
The truth spoken in love is the wound of a friend

The Day After

The impulse to sin within you is strong
Your flesh is in control you no longer discern right from wrong
In the heat of the moment you blindly follow the throng
What will you do the day after?

At that moment in time you'd do anything to satisfy your lust
You'd lie, cheat, or steal, you're way beyond trust
What started out as pleasure has now become a must
What will you do the day after?

"Watch who you hang out with", your parents have told you
But you got it all figured out, they can't tell you what to do
Your buddies knocked over a liquor store now you're talking to the men in blue
What will you do the day after?

Your mother told you to wait until marriage to have sex
But his smile just melts you and you get weak when his muscles flex
When you told him you're pregnant he said "Not mine" then hollers next
What will you do the day after?

You stop on the way home just to have a little drink
The more alcohol you consume the less rational you think
If you'd only called a cab you wouldn't be sitting in the clink
What will you do the day after?

Your friend tried to talk to you about the Lord Jesus Christ
You said, "I don't have time for religion, I live a good life"
Now you're on the other side of eternity and where you're at isn't so nice
What will you do the day after?

Womb Tomb

The Lord knew the number of my days
Before the very first
My entire life lay before Him
Even before my scheduled birth
He knew me and He loved me
As I was formed in that secret place
The place He created for the survival of the human race
God's purpose was for me to live
To be part of His eternal plan
But my life was taken before my birth
By the selfishness of man
Although I was conceived on God's schedule
His timing didn't work for you
My conception was an inconvenience
Because you had other things you wanted to do
"I'm too young to have a baby!"
"This can't be happening to me!"
"What will my mother and father say?"
So you search for a remedy
"Having this baby is out of the question!"
"Besides, I can't raise it alone!"
Your boyfriend threatens to leave you
If you don't pick up that phone
You're nervous and you're scared
But it seems like the only way
You call Clinic on the phone
They schedule you that very day
Your boyfriend starts to calm down
He assures you that he'll pay the fee
"Baby, in a little while it'll be over and then we'll be free!"
As you lay on that cold, hard table
Doubts go through your mind
You wonder if you made a mistake
Maybe you should come back another time

Maybe you should talk this over with your parents
They never let you down before
You hear the echo of footsteps on the shiny ceramic floor
A strange man enters the room
He assures you it'll be over in a bit
Your mind tells you to leave right now
But your body won't let you quit
"Relax; it will soon be over,
He says with a toothy smile
As he walks out the door he waves and says,
"The nurse will see you in a little while!"
As you lay on the table waiting
The tears flow from your eyes
You feel like you've done something awful
You think you hear your lost baby cries
You thought that in your life
For a baby there was no room
You changed the chamber meant for life
Into your baby's tomb

Choices

Don't you realize the damage that's been done to me
Because of the choices you made so ignorantly
You could not wait until you left home
You felt too confined, you wanted to roam
As a child you were taught what being a child of God means
And you knew the consequences disobedience brings
You wanted to do things your way, you wanted to be free
Never realizing the damage your choices done to me
You were taught how to resist the enemy
But your flesh took control in your desire to be free
Do you know who it is that speaks to you?
You'll know exactly who I am before I'm through
Every choice you made I was right there
And I'm telling you now that it isn't fair
You could have done so much more with your life
Then I wouldn't be living in a home full of fear and strife
If you made better choices you could have been so much further along
Instead of living in this pit that we call home
Every choice you make, everything you do
Have consequences for others besides you
The choices you make are serious indeed
Every choice you make affects your unborn seed
Make your choices with purpose and not just for fun
The choices you make affect future generations
Think carefully about everything you do
You unborn children are depending on you

Mom, please make good choices, in God you must trust
Please don't make selfish choices, please think about us

Signed,

Your Unborn Children

A Double-Minded Man

In the presence of light the darkness must flee
How can light and darkness both inhabit me?
Sometimes hot, sometimes cold, sometimes shy, sometimes bold
Doing good one moment and evil the next
I must admit that I'm perplexed
How can this be? I just don't understand
How can blessings and curses come out the same man?
When it comes to church attendance I am really good
As the head of my home I don't always do as I should
A double-minded man is unstable in all his ways
How can such a person receive from the Lord when he prays?
Are you of the truth or a liar in sin?
Do you change your clothes because of the company you're in?
When you talk to the pastor you're as cute as pie
But when you talk to your wife you make her cry
You're very patient with your children in a public place
But when you get them in private you wear a different face
You put time in at the shelter to feed the homeless bread
While your next door neighbor goes unfed
You know about the truth and the consequences of sin
But you won't talk about Jesus with your unsaved friends
This hot and cold, light and dark just won't do
You must stay on course if you want to breakthrough
Every time you step forward you take a step back
You'll never take ground from the enemy if you don't sustain the attack
The need to renew your mind is very clear
The first enemy to overcome is the one called fear
The next enemy is the love of earthly things
You don't want all the trouble that the love of the world brings
If this poem is a mirror and you see your face
Get on your knees, repent and ask for mercy and grace
There's no sin so dirty that Jesus' Blood can't cleanse
Go to those you've offended and make amends

Now the truth of the gospel is right before your eyes
You're no longer deceived by the enemy's lies

There's a Rebel in the House

A disobedient child plays you against your spouse
This is an indication that there's a rebel in the house
You have an employee who won't do things your way
It's very easy for a rebel to ruin your day
You have a church member spreading slander about the pastor
When a rebel leaves an area it looks like a disaster
A rebel won't submit to authority
That's why life is always hard for them you see
They sow so much bad until their number is up
Then when it's time to reap they drink from the bitter cup
A rebel won't submit to her manager
Then wonders why her children won't obey her
A rebellious child causes trouble in their home
Then when he turns 18 he wonders why he's all alone
A rebellious wife exposes the secrets of her house
Then wonders how that harlot got next to her spouse
A rebellious husband refuses to submit to God
Then wonders why his family life is so hard
A rebellious church member tries to bring the pastor down
Then wonders why nobody ever wants them around
If you have a problem submitting to those appointed over you
You also have a problem with the One who placed them over you
All rebellion is ultimately directed against God
Rebels live in parched lands and barren roads they trod
If anything in this poem sounds like you
Then this is what you ought to do
Ask God to give you a servant's heart
So from your rebellious ways you can depart
Serve all authority as if you're serving Him
Respect the position because God is the One who chose them
You now know what to look for be a man and not a mouse
To keep your ship smoothly sailing get the rebel out the house

Who's Your Ruler?

Darkness cannot coexist with light
A choice cannot be both wrong and right
No man can serve two masters
He will always hate one and love the other
You cannot love God if you don't love your brother

When you meditate upon sin it's the same as committing the act
Speaking evil of others hurts as much as a physical attack
People tend to think more highly of themselves than they ought
When evil is directed toward you, you consider it to be a crime
But if you judged yourself rightly you would see that you do it all the time

What I meditate on becomes a seed in my mind
Wheat and tares look the same until the fullness of time
How can you discern right from wrong unless you know God's Word
You cannot discern the difference between wrong and right
If you fellowship with darkness and shun His Light

You made a decision to give your life to the Lord Jesus Christ
God has given you the power to resist sin so you can do what's right
But the sin that you tolerate in your life spreads like a weed
Sin put Jesus on the cross and tried to put out His Light
Sin will also try to crucify Jesus in your life

When Jesus saved you, that was it; it's over; it's done
He did all the work; He doesn't need your contribution
The only things you need do are trust and believe
And together with Him there's so much you'll achieve
Wake up from your stupor you lost wayward saint!
Quit your crying and moaning and constant complains!
Why can't you see what Jesus has done?

Why can't you see the Victorious One?
Seductive demons work hard to entice you to defect
In Jesus' name you should have your foot on their neck
Jesus said, "In My name cast out demons and speak in new tongues"
If you've been baptized and believe then you've already won
Jesus lives on the inside of you
Crucify sin or it will crucify you
Jesus or sin, it's now time to choose
Will you live as a victor and continue being abused?
Stop wandering through life as if you are lost
Walk with sure steps and show Satan who's the boss

Your Works Reveal Your Faith

For indeed we have had good news preached to us, just as they also; but the word they heard did not profit them, because it was not united by faith in those who heard. Hebrews 4:2

And all ate the same spiritual food; and all drank the same spiritual drink, for they were drinking from a spiritual rock which followed them; and the rock was Christ. Nevertheless, with most of them God was not well-pleased for they were laid low in the wilderness. 1 Corinthians 10:3-5

Faith: Such knowledge of, assent to, and confidence in certain divine truths, especially those of the Gospel, as produces good works.

It takes more than the Word to get the results of the Word. The Word must be united by faith.

WORD + FAITH = RESULTS

But are you willing to recognize you foolish fellows that faith without works is useless? James 2:20

For in Christ Jesus neither circumcision nor uncircumcision means anything, but faith working through love. Galatians 5:6

The Word are the instructions, faith is acting on those instructions. If I believe something to be true I will demonstrate my belief with a corresponding act. For example, if I believe a chair will support my weight I will sit on it. If I doubt, I won't.

Integrity: the quality of being honest and having strong moral principles; the state of being whole and undivided, the

condition of being unified, unimpaired, or sound in construction.

Faith is not based upon the words heard but on the trustworthiness of the speaker. When you fail to act upon the instructions, directions, or advice given to you, you are not rejecting the words, but the person who spoke them. Disobedience to parents demonstrates a lack of trust in their integrity. Likewise, disobedience to the Lord demonstrates a lack of trust in the integrity of God.

Professed faith without corresponding action is not faith at all. People don't pray because they don't have faith in God. People don't forgive because they don't have faith in God. People disobey the Word because they don't have faith in God. If the only faith you profess is faith that you are saved and not going to hell, if that is the only faith you can demonstrate, do you really even possess that faith? Are you only hoping that that one time confession was for real? Is it possible to trust God with something as consequential as eternal salvation and not with daily living? Only you can answer that question.

Not everyone who says to Me, 'Lord, Lord' will enter the kingdom of heaven; but he who does the will on My Father who is in heaven. Matthew 7:21

If you love the Lord you'll obey His commands
This is not a request, it's what He demands
A tree is known by its fruit
A good tree producing bad fruit doesn't compute
Everyone misses it from time to time
You fall down, repent, and then continue to climb
Everyone commits an occasional sin
You fall out of fellowship and then come back in
But if you willingly choose a lifestyle of iniquity
Believing that a one-time confession is your guarantee

Of going to heaven and escaping hell
You should examine yourself very well
Jesus said, "Why do you call Me Lord, Lord and don't do what I say?"
You come to church on Sunday, but live like the devil every other day
You think that you're safe because you put in your hour each week
Your flesh is very strong and your spirit is very weak
You say, "Lord, look at all I have done in Your Name"
But your works reveal your faith, you bring Him nothing but shame
You claim to be a Christian, a soldier in the Lord's Army
But your works reveal that you're an agent of the enemy
You change the truth of God into a lie
When things don't work out you wonder why?
You say that you love Him, but you don't trust the Lord
If you trusted Him you would repent and get back on board
Faith is trusting so much it generate a corresponding act
Who you trust reveals your faith, this is a documented fact
The Lord says, "Love your enemy!" You say, "Not today!"
You say, "An eye for an eye, that's how it's played"
The Lord says, "Forgive others their faults or I won't forgive you"
You say, "I'll never forgive what they did to me, this conversation is through"
From out of your heart flow the issues of life
Your lifestyle reveals whether you serve Satan or Jesus Christ
You faith is revealed by the choices you make
You look like a lamb, but you live like a snake
The Book of Jude speaks about those who live as you do
Read on to see if God's Word accurately describes you
Indulging in gross immorality, seeking strange flesh
You fornicate and commit adultery; your life is a mess
Hidden reefs at the love banquet, fellowshipping without fear
Clouds without water, doubly dead, you have ears but can't hear
Grumblers, finding fault, following your own lusts
Speaking arrogantly, flattering people, trying to gain their trust

Causing divisions, worldly-minded, devoid of the Spirit too
Coming to church for the wrong reasons trying to take advantage of you
The time for excuses is over; it's time that you realized
That you cannot continue living a double life, your existence is a lie
Your faith is demonstrated by your works by now this should be clear
Accept the Lord with your whole heart its Him you should reverently fear

"And why do you call Me 'Lord, Lord,' and do not do what I say?"
Luke 6:46

Small Acts of Disobedience

Just like a ship that slips loose from the shore
Recovering from small acts of disobedience can be a big chore
Not that it's hard to get back to where you need to be
But your ability to hear has been impaired you see
Every time the Lord speaks to you and you refuse to obey
Just like a cat stalking a mouse you're being set-up as prey
There are temptations all around us that pull on our flesh
Failure to pray and stay in the Word keeps us from entering His Rest
We used to look for those spare moments in order to pray
But now we do other things to occupy ourselves during the day
Who you fellowship with you eventually become like
Do you fellowship with darkness or dwell in His Light?
Some of us try to live in both worlds but we pay a hefty fee
Salt and fresh water from one opening reveal my inconsistencies
As we slowly we drift away from our First Love
We cut ourselves off from the power of the Lord above
It's time to make a decision, who sits on the throne of your life?
Is self calling the shots or the Lord Jesus Christ?
If you have drifted into uncharted waters and there's no shore in sight
Small acts of obedience will show you the way back to His Light

How Long?

How long, you simpletons, will you insist on being simpleminded? How long will you mockers relish your mocking? How long will you fools hate knowledge? Proverbs 1:22

When they cry for help, I will not answer. Though they anxiously search for me, they will not find me. For they hated knowledge and chose not to fear the Lord. They rejected my advice and paid no attention when I corrected them. Therefore, they must eat the bitter fruit of living their own way. Choking on their own schemes. Proverbs 1:28-31

Those who seek their own wills and only want to play
Separate from those who can show them the right way
Those who reject truth and follow after what is false
One day will have to give an account and pay a very high cost
No one has all the answers, we can't go it alone
God provides teachers and mentors until we're spiritually grown
The Bible calls us sheep because without a Shepherd we cannot survive
When we separate and ignore sound instruction we have a problem with pride
God uses teachers, preachers, friends and books to impart knowledge to you
You can lead a horse to water, but can't make him drink; it's up to you to follow-through
You ignore all sound advice because you believe that what you're doing is right
Not realizing that you're walking in the darkness of Satan's false light
Deception comes much easier when you're separated from those who love you
If the enemy can cut off the voices of reason he can more easily control you

It breaks my heart to see you make choices that are leading you away from God
You're blind and can't see and your choices have scheduled a hard road for you to trod

You will say, "How I hated discipline! If only I had not ignored all the warnings! Oh, why didn't I listen to my teachers? Why didn't I pay attention to my instructors?" Proverbs 5:12-13

How Could You Say All The Things That You Do?

How could you say all the things that you do?
When we've shown nothing but love for you
You pretend that everything is O.K.
But around others you act a different way

All your life you have been catering to men
Always thinking that you had the upper hand
Doing anything to get next to them
Responding to their every whim
Sacrificing time with your child
Just to get a man to give you a smile
You neglected and left your child all alone
When you should have been with her at home

How could you say all the things that you do?
When we've shown nothing but love for you

When your Ex threw you out of your home
You were desperate and felt so all alone
He violated all your marriage vows
But you are the other woman now
He really hurt you deep within
Adultery is a carnal sin
The other woman upset your happy home
Now you're the adulterer and your sin is well known

How could you say all the things that you do?
When we've shown nothing but love for you

When you needed a place to stay
We opened our home and provided you a way
We covered all your expenses but this you already knew

We suffered financially while your bank account grew
Many times we couldn't make ends meet
And we thought we would go down in defeat
We thought that we were one family
But when it came to helping out you were an absentee

How could you say all the things that you do?
When we've shown nothing but love for you

Your grandchildren live in the same home as you
But they hardly spend any time with you
Every weekend you go out of town
It doesn't bother them that you're not around
You always have time for others, but not for them
You only spend time when you start to feel condemned
You won't even take the time to do their hair
So we have to get it done elsewhere

How could you say all the things that you do?
When we've shown nothing but love for you

Your only priority is me, myself, and I
Many times we asked ourselves, why?
You were selfish before and you still are today
I think it's time that we went our separate ways
It's obvious that you don't care about us
A two-faced person is someone you just can't trust

How could you say all the things that you do?
When we've shown nothing but love for you

You try to portray yourself as a winner
But everyone knows that you're just a pretender
You talk real big when no one is around
But face to face you start to breakdown
We opened our home and hearts to you

But you used and abused all the love we had for you
You've been dragging our names through the dirt
We want you to know that betrayal really hurts

How could you say all the things that you do?
When we've shown nothing but love for you

Stop Drifting

You forgave all my debts; You washed away all my sins
You died on a cross at Calvary so I could enter in
You rescued me from the authority of the devil
The scales were unbalanced but now they are level
You are my Lord, the Giver of grace
You + me = there's nothing I can't face
Here I now stand a man without a past
The Blood washed away my sins I'm no longer an outcast
The anointing here, the anointing there, I've traveled all over the country
Blind and ignorant to the fact that You live in me
The problem is You are in one room and I am in another
I'm so busy doing my own thing that we don't fellowship with each other
A husband and wife live at the same address
Day after day it seems they're going through a test
The solution to their problem is easy to see
They never take time to reestablish intimacy
They are so focused on all the things that they have to do
That they never take the time to cuddle and say; "I love you!"
They're so busy ministering outside that they neglect to minister within
Lack of intimacy opens the way to sin to enter in
Because you're overwhelmed by all the things you have to do
You've drifted apart and now you don't know what to do
It's time to say "Time Out"; it's time to put some things on hold
It's time to be calculating, persistent, and bold
It's time to reconnect with the one you love
The same is true of your intimacy with the Lord Above
Where you spend your time show the values in your life
Don't say you love the Lord when you don't spend time with your wife
You're doing good works but you're neglecting your home
The Lord and your spouse you've left all alone

Tell them that you love them and you hold them both dear
Unashamedly expressing your love without hesitancy or fear
Don't give them leftovers only give them your best
Intimacy with the one you love will help you through a test

The People Test
(Who are you trying to impress?)

(Your private life is your reputation with God. Your public life is your reputation with people)

Cursed is the man who trusts in flesh
His life is troubled and he has no rest
Trying to be pleasing in others eyes
Is a snare and a trap, it's very unwise
Saul, the first king of Israel, heads and shoulders above the rest
Time and time again this man failed the People Test
He let the opinion of people sway him from the will of God
As a result of the choices he made a rough road he had to trod
God gave him another chance to redeem himself in His sight
He sent him on a mission to destroy the Amaletkes
God told him to spare nothing, to wipe them off the face of the earth
Obedience brings a blessing, disobedience brings a curse
Saul allowed the people to turn his heart
From obedience to the Lord he did depart
God became angry and took the kingdom from him
He gave it to another who would obey and worship Him
Satan will use people to keep you in place
If you value their opinion more than God you'll go down in disgrace
God will sometimes place you in situations to initiate change
Your obedience to the Lord may appear to others strange
Many saints never fulfill the call of God on their life
They allow people to intimidate them and keep them in strife
The best place to be is "God, I can't do this alone!"
"If You won't go with me, just leave me at home"
Dependence on the Lord eliminates the need for the approval of man
When others say you can't, the Lord says you can
If man places you in a position, he can also remove you from it

God tells you to go forward, man tells you to quit
Obey the Lord, don't fear man
He'll make it His business to see that you stand
Trying to please the people takes you out of His rest
Compromise will always lead you into a mess
When you were small in your own eyes you trusted in Him
Now that you have position and power you want to appear legitimate to them
When it was just you and God nobody else was there
Now that He has blessed you the people say that they care
When you are popular you have many friends
When trouble strikes few will be there till the end
The people's opinions change from day to day
Trying to keep them pleased will detour you from His Way
"Lord, forgive me, for I have sinned against You"
"Fear of man has caused me to compromise against You"
"I ignored Your witness, and allowed the people to lead me astray"
"I've been disobedient to You Lord, and now I've lost my way"
"Restore to me Lord, all that I have lost"
"I realize how much fearing man has really cost"
"Remove from me fear, and remove from me shame"
"Lord speak and remind me of my new covenant names"
Cursed is the man who trusts in flesh
Many have gone home without passing the People Test

Living a Double Life

You work all week waiting for the weekend
You work all week waiting for the fun to begin
Friday night is when the party starts
The drudgery of working all week will soon depart
Sunday morning you wake up hung over from the night before
You got to go to church; it's just one of many chores
When you're at church you serve in ministry faithfully
But when you're on your job you complain constantly
You sit in the pew screaming and clapping your hands
But your mind is really on the night before when you danced to the band
No one can serve two masters; you'll love one and hate the other
You're sinning all week then on Sunday you sit next to your brother
You're living a double life and your witness isn't good
It's time to forsake your wicked ways and start living, as you should
Your life isn't a witness of what your mouth confesses
Because you're sowing bad seeds you go through many tests
You go church and there are things you would never do or say
But your body is His temple and you defile it everyday
It's time to wake up and forsake your sins
Turn from your evil ways and enjoy His fellowship again
Where sin abounds there's much more grace available to you
The Most High God will do a mighty work in you
It's time to stop living a double life
And give your whole heart to the Lord Jesus Christ

Practice What You Preach

But if you bear the name "Jew; and rely upon the Law, and boast in God, and <u>know His will,</u> and approve the things that are essential, being instructed out of the Law, and are confident that you yourself are a guide to the blind, a light to those who are in darkness, a corrector of the foolish, a teacher of the immature, having in the Law the embodiment of knowledge and truth, you therefore, who teach another, do you not teach yourself? You who preach that one should not commit adultery, do you commit adultery? You who abhor idols, do you rob temples? You who boast in the Law, through your breaking the Law, do you dishonor God? For the name of God is blasphemed among the Gentiles because of you," just as it is written. Romans 2:17-24

You are deceived and close to being cursed
If you put Jesus second and other things first
Although your spirit is reborn, your mind is unrenewed
A house divided can't stand, how can you be used?
With your mouth you profess to love God, but your life is a mess
You think you are spiritual because you go through many tests
The trials you've been through are because of your undisciplined life
You gossip, complain, refuse to give, and don't live in harmony with you wife
You're more interested in having your rights than letting your light shine
Then you're wondering why you're experiencing loss time after time
If you were hot or cold then something could be done with you
But you are lukewarm and you think you're okay, but the story isn't through
Your mission is to re-present Jesus while you're on the Earth
This commission was given to you before the day of your birth

Whose character is being displayed as you go through your daily walk?
The Lord expects more out of you than just a lot of empty talk
It's the doer, not the hearer who is blessed; you know this to be true
You've got the Bible memorized from cover to cover so what's the matter with you?
God has sent you among people who are supposed to see your light
When they see Jesus in the way you live the falsehood is exposed by what's right
You will be held accountable for what you know but do not do
It's one thing to be doubtful, but disobedience is unbecoming to you
It's insanity to keep doing the same things expecting different results
It's time to stop acting like children and starts being adults
What we are we reproduce; the change must start in us first
Your unwillingness to change causes your children to be cursed
Think about all the things that you had to go through
Do you want your children to go through the same things too?
Practice what you preach and always do what's right
Don't let sin and disobedience cover your light
You have the advantage of seeing cause and effect, you know wrong from right
If you allow God to renew your mind your children will live a better life
It's better to judge yourself than for God to judge you
It's time to deal with the sin which so easily snares and entraps you
It's time to measure your life against the Word of the Lord
It's time to stop compromising and be freed from sin's cords
It's time to stop looking for exceptions and loopholes in the Word of God
It's time to admit to ourselves and God it's our fault we're on the hard road we trod

It's time to stop denying the literalness of the Word when our lives don't look the same
It's time to reject the old titles and start living up to our new names
It's time to locate ourselves so we can be found and get back on track
It's time to start admitting that maybe it's our fault we're under attack
It's time to stop being unproductive like a whale that is beached
It's time to start practicing what's in the Word; there are so many people to reach
You have an assignment; you have the playbook, now engage the enemy
People are looking at you; you're placed where you are so they can be free

Praise Him in Tough Times

God never promised that following Him would be an easy chore
Opportunities and obstacles are waiting just beyond that open door
You are an arrow in the Lord's quiver He determines where you will go
Wherever He leads needs must be met and you will face off with a foe
Every place you tread will be contested but you have the victory
The devil uses people to accomplish his will, but they are not your enemy
The world lies in the power of the devil like puppets on a string
They cannot resist his will; he makes them do despicable things
One day you're witnessing for the Lord, the next day you're in jail
One day you're mounted up on wings like eagle, the next day you're in a cell
"All I did was obey the Lord and set the captives free"
"And now I'm sitting in a pit chained and in captivity"
The atmosphere that surrounds you attracts or repels spiritual things
God inhabits the praises of His people, unthankfulness brings demonic beings
No matter how securely you are bound pray and sing praises to God
I'll guarantee that He can overcome any kind of odds
Death and life are in the power of the tongue, those who love it will eat its fruit
Speaking one thing and expecting another just does not compute
You are a soldier of the Lord and enemies you will face
Preparation before confrontation will keep you focused and in the race
You must spend time in the secret place before you engage the enemy
When you're engaged it's not the time to reexamine your theology
Just because the enemy is invisible doesn't mean they aren't real

You better know who Jesus is before you charge down off that hill
Do you expect everything to rosy and comfortable in this life?
Do you think you'll never be around difficult people and have to deal with strife?
Do you think because you're a Christian you'll never experience lack?
Do you think that you'll live on this earth and never come under attack?
Do you think you'll never be shunned and hated by man?
Do you think there'll never be a circumstance in which you have to stand?
Do you think there'll never be times when you're battling with fear?
Do you think there'll never be times when you have to shed a tear?
Do you think you'll always have peace and never have to war?
Do you think there'll never be times you have to pick yourself off the floor?
When you go through tough times can you still believe God?
Can you continue walking in faith when every step you take is hard?
When you're hard at work and everyone else is out at play
Can you raise your hands in praise and thank Him anyway?
When darkness surrounds you and your vision is dim
Will you trust the Lord and continue to follow Him?
Trials and tribulations are the proving ground for your faith
When you receive revelation you and the enemy have a date
The enemy won't give up ground without a fight
So you better be sure that you're walking in the light
Like gold in a furnace you're becoming more pure
If you abide in Christ your victory is sure

Strange Place

I never thought I would be in this place
When I first decided to enter the race
I've been through trials and tribulations before
But this battle has shaken me to my very core
I've seen the miraculous things You have done in the past
But Lord I feel like I'm running out of gas
I'm constantly plummeted and pounded day after day
Why don't You respond when I kneel down to pray?
I know that You hear me there's no doubt about that
But why do You remain silent while I am being attacked?
I've prayed and cried so much I don't know what to do
If You don't show up soon I know that I'm through
So here I am today in this strange place
Hoping somehow to see your face
All throughout history your people have gone through trials
Sometimes they passed through quickly sometimes it took a while
But in the end You always came through
When they forsook their sins and returned back to You

Sometimes the Godly Must Fall!

There are people in your life who fellowship with division and strife
When they enter a situation peace departs, this is their lot in life
They continually make bad choices and others are affected by them
They will not act upon the advice you give but want you to rescue them
A wise man will hear and heed, a fool continues on his way
They ignore godly counsel then suffer for it at the end of the day
Their pride is their downfall, they're slaves to their vice
The choices they make demonstrate that they are far from Jesus Christ
The Pastor teaches a word that convicts you to your core
By the time you make it home you're doing the same things you were before
You go to your friends for counsel and they give good advice to you
But you ignore the advice they give because you want to do what you want to do
You make life changing decisions without counting the cost
You're like a ship on stormy seas that's continually being tossed
When the inevitable happens and you suffer great loss
You go back to those who tried to warn you and want them to cover the cost
This becomes your pattern; you do it over and over again
When someone speaks the truth to you you're so easy to offend
You separate from your loved ones to do things your own way
Then when your life is falling apart you want your loved ones to pay
Life and death, blessings and curses, God set these paths before you
Your life is a mess because you ignore the Word and do what you want to do

Sometimes the best motivator for change is to feel the pain in your flesh
People will not continue to rescue you from the end of your test
People who continually rescue others from the pain of their choice
Position themselves in the place of God and keep others from hearing His voice
As much as it sometimes hurt to see your loved ones fall
If you continually become their safety net you'll soon see their life stall
Their life cannot progress past the point where you rescue them
You prevent them from learning the life lesson that God wants to teach them
You know who the people are in your life that will not follow godly advice
Because they walk in a direction far away from the Lord Jesus Christ
They fellowship with darkness and shun the light, facing one crisis after another
They're stubborn, prideful and refuse to listen to godly counsel from others
Their choices place them in bad situations
They attend class but never make it to graduation
They will take your money but not your advice
Their choices write a check but they want you to pay the price
If you let them feel the pain of their choice
Then maybe they can start to hear God's voice

No Pain, No Gain

It was good that I was stricken
For my affliction revealed to me
How far away I had drifted
From the path You set for me

I thought nothing was wrong
Everything seemed to be O.K.
But the flow just wasn't there
When I knelt down to pray

I was going through the motions
Attending church each week
But my focus it was broken
Because Your face I ceased to seek

You became an afterthought
There were so many other things to do
But when I encountered trouble
Somehow I found the time for You

Other things caught my attention
From different streams I quenched my thirst
Other things became my priority
My first love was no longer first

It was good that I was afflicted
The pain revealed there was no fruit
Other things caught my attention
You were no longer my chief pursuit

Because You are so long suffering
I took your grace for granted
I thought I was O.K.
But I was totally disenchanted

Every time I got into trouble
I would bow my head and pray
You're so Good, You're so Faithful
You would always save the day

Thank You Lord for opening my eyes
Thank You for taking the darkness away
Now that I realize my error
When You speak I will obey

Priorities

You are My brothers if you obey Me when I call
Rejecting My Word to please others will surely cause you to fall
I called you out of the world for this reason
So you can begin life anew, you're in a new season
It's time to shed the old and put on the new
It's time to stop doing the things that you used to do
I must be the first love in your life
Your second love should be your husband or wife
It's time for you to forsake your former ways
Yesterday is gone and today is a brand new day
I called you out from among your family
I freed you from a spiritual captivity
It's time to disconnect from the sins of your family
Behold, I'm about to reveal a great mystery
Your problems are rooted in a generational curse
You reject truth when My Word is second and your family comes first
Submit to your husband and be a good wife
If you obey Me you'll live the abundant life
As a man, you're the head of your family
It's your job to protect them from the enemy
You should be the chief servant in your home
Many times you'll feel unappreciated and alone
You're not called to quit, but to fight the good fight
Your chief desire should be to constantly remain in My Light
I will speak to you and give you direction for all
If you obey My Word you'll never fall
On the backs of people is how the enemy gets in
You must work together in order to defend
The Lord will manifest in a home filled with peace
If strife is in your home command it to cease
The place of agreement is the place of power
It's time to work together for this is your hour

How Long Will You Waver?

Then Elijah stood in front of them and said, "How long are you going to waver between two opinions? If the Lord is God, follow Him! But if Baal is God, then follow him!" But the people were completely silent.
1 Kings 18:21

Today, let the Church of Jesus Christ rise up and say, "How long are you going to waver between two opinions? If a fetus is a human protect them! But if a fetus is not human destroy them! But as the debate raged on the Church was silent.

You can't have it both ways
You must choose one or the other
How can you say a child isn't human?
Just because he's inside his mother
Society has surely gone crazy
People just don't have a clue
The laws are so ambiguous
No one knows what to do
A woman can abort her baby
And it isn't considered a crime
If someone else kills her unborn child
That person will have to do time

There once was a lady who no longer wanted her child
She tried to induce an abortion, but became frustrated after a while
She enlisted the help of her boyfriend, because she couldn't do it alone
He beat her stomach until the baby died; the child was cold as stone
The boyfriend was arrested and charged with murder in the first degree

The woman walked, because the law says she has a right to kill her own baby
How can this be justified, the end result is the same
A child was murdered; he left this world, without even a name
It's time for complacency to end
We can no longer turn a blind eye
When we stand before the throne of God
We'll have to give an account; Why?
Why did we remain silent as innocent blood was shed?
Why did we hide in our churches and ignore the cries of the dead?
Why were we afraid to stand up to a hostile society?
Why didn't we speak the truth in love for all the world to see?
Like Elijah your voice may be the only one in a multitude of opposing opinions
If you trust in the Lord and do what is right, He will cover you with His pinions
With God on your side you have nothing at all to fear
He loves and holds these innocent ones very dear
Will you speak up for those who cannot speak for themselves?
Are you willing to put it all on the line, or will you put your faith on the shelf?
We have our own prophets of Baal that we must face
It's time to stop hiding in fear; it's time to get back in the race

Let Go of the Pride

I'm in a bad place and don't feel I can advance
My joy is gone and I'm overwhelmed by my circumstance
The pressure is building and I don't know how much more I can take
I wish that I could leave all this mess and just take a break
I'm the man of the house and everyone's depending on me
But I know that I'm not at the place that I should be
Trying to fight this battle in my own strength
I can barely walk and I'm totally spent
Pride always comes before a fall
I need some help, but who can I call?
I'm supposed to be a man
My family's depending on me
My house is falling apart because my wife and I cannot agree
On where we're going or what we should do
We're like two blind men in a ditch without a clue
How can I call my friends when I'm supposed to be a man?
Pride keeps me from seeking help when I know that I can't stand

Let go of the pride and start to abide
Worship the Lord from the heart
Let the Holy Spirit lead and guide

You don't have all the answers
You don't even have a clue
Stop thinking more highly of yourself than you ought too
First acknowledge that you're lost and don't have a clue
Seek the Lord with all your might that is what you need to do
Ask the Holy Spirit to reveal to you
If there's anything within you that needs ministering to
As He speaks you must obey
Change normally takes more than one day
Resolve to do His will no matter what you're going through
As you submit to His Will you will soon see your breakthrough

God is more concerned about the condition of your soul
Than in the things you possess
There's a place in God even in the midst of war
That you can walk in His Rest
God allows difficult circumstances to come into your life
He uses everything to conform you into the image of Jesus Christ

Let go of the pride and start to abide
Worship the Lord from the heart
Let the Holy Spirit lead and guide

Don't Give In To Fear

All your life you followed the crowd
Cloning the latest trends made you feel real proud
Amongst the trees in the garden you are hidden in the midst
Herded and maneuvered by others opinions, you think you are in bliss
Afraid to step out and be your own man
Afraid to live by principles and take a stand
Afraid to boldly go where no man has gone before
You'll never reach the stars if your feet don't leave the floor
You want to be a trailblazer, leading others to new frontiers
But you will not take the next step because you're bound by fear
Living by the world's standards has brought you nothing but trouble
When you hit rock bottom you run to the Lord on the double

You make the journey over from death to life
Because Jesus gave His life as a sacrifice
Your spirit is reborn and now all things are new
But old habits will not die until your mind is renewed

You're still following the crowd, and hiding amongst the trees
You cry out in prayer, "Lord, deliver me please!"
Still afraid to step out and be your own man
When others compromise you refuse to take a stand
Afraid to boldly go where no man has gone before
Revelation is denied because your feet won't leave the shore

As you continue to pray and fellowship with Him a change comes over you
*In "**your experience**" old things are passing away and behold all things are new*
Love replaces fear and you have boldness like never before
The revelation of "Christ in You" rocks you to your core
Chickens stay together in coops; eagles soar high in the skies

You feel safe with the crowd, but it's time to say goodbye
You will draw persecution when you are a pioneer
But you must be obedient and not give in to fear

Eleven stayed in the boat, but one stepped out in faith
One obstacle to instant obedience is when we hesitate
One walked on the water, eleven stayed in the boat
To do what God tells you to do you must walk in faith not hope
Ten spies gave an evil report, two said let's take the land
Even when others compromise you must continue to stand
Goliath held Israel hostage, each man hiding in his tent
Others were afraid to face the giant but faithful David went
Gideon was afraid of the Midianites, so he hid in the wine press
And when the angel of the Lord appeared to him he put him to the test
When the angel came to Gideon he was the wimp of his family
But God did a mighty work in him and he brought Israel the victory
God appeared to Noah and told him to build a big boat
In obedience Noah built it by faith, his flesh didn't get a vote
He endured ridicule because he did something never done before
But the mockers weren't laughing when the rain fell and he shut the door
Esther was the chosen queen, another example of faith
She lived in the lap of luxury on the royal estate
Her uncle Mordecai gave her some very bad news
Haman the Agagite was trying to kill off all the Jews
He told her she may have raised up for such a time as this
By faith she talked to the king and was not dismissed

You'll never possess what you are believing for until you pass the test
Faith without works is dead, you must do more than confess
Apart from God you can do nothing, let me make this very clear
You're in covenant with the Most High God perfect love casts out fear
Just because you are a pioneer and it's never been done before

Means this is your assignment, your God given chore
Sometimes living by faith can be a lonely walk
The chosen will step out in faith, the called mostly talk
When God calls you out from amongst the others
You'll sometimes draw persecution from your brothers
Walk in instant obedience and don't give in to fear
You're not in this alone for God is always near

Come Back Home

Judgment is floating all around
Looking for a place to settle down
The natural result of the works of the flesh
Many a good Saint has been put to the test
We are to pray always and be watchful besides
Because the attacks usually hits you from the blind side
The attacks are so subtle and comes in degrees
That pretty soon your flesh is doing whatever it pleases
Be on your guard and always pray
Don't become lukewarm and start to drift away
If the heat is turned up slowly, I'll stay until I'm boiled alive
But if it's turned up suddenly, the pain drives me to survive
Remember when you looked forward to going to church to pray?
But now you have better things to do with your day
Studying your Bible used to give you such a thrill
Now you seek other things to keep you fulfilled
You used to walk after the Spirit instead of the flesh
Now you're working harder and producing less
Covered by the Blood was the place you once dwelled
You have forsaken your First Love, now you're going through hell
You lost sight of who you were, and came out of His Light
Now you find yourself outmatched, in the fight of your life
Separated from the sheepfold surrounded by wild beasts
There's lust in their eyes, and on your flesh they want to feast
Remember who you are and who you belong too
He's never been very far; He's always been with you
Don't wait a moment longer make a quality decision today
Repent of your sin, drop to your knees, and start to pray
The Lord is faithful to forgive you, and remove all sin
Don't be like the prodigal, and stay too long in the pig pen
Come back to your Father, He's been waiting for you
He has a robe, a ring, and a fatted calf too
You can come back home today, without a question being asked

Now that you're forgiven, today's your present; you're a man without a past

Don't Go Back

And all ate the same spiritual food; and all drank the same spiritual drink, for they were drinking from a spiritual rock which followed them; and the rock was Christ. Nevertheless, with most of them God was not well-pleased; for they were laid low in the wilderness. Now these things happened as examples for us, that we should not crave evil things, as they also craved. And do not be idolaters, as some of them were; as it is written, "The people sat down to eat and drink, and stood up to play." Nor let us act immorally, as some of them did, and twenty-three thousand fell in one day. Nor let us try the Lord, as some of them did, and were destroyed by the serpents. Nor grumble, as some of them did, and were destroyed by the destroyer. 1 Corinthians 10:3-10

"For which one of you, when he wants to build a tower, does not first sit down and calculate the cost, to see if he has enough to complete it? Otherwise when he has laid a foundation, and is not able to finish, all who observe it begin to ridicule him, saying, 'This man began to build and was not able to finish.'" Luke 14:28-30

You used to live in Egypt and worked like a slave
Controlled by a taskmaster, who was cruel and depraved
You struggled through life with no hope at all
Every time you gained momentum your life would stall
In Egypt, you drank, drugged, and partied all night
You worshipped strange gods and shunned His Light
You struggled each day to make ends meets
Your heart was dark and evil; you were a liar and a cheat
You didn't have anyone who you could truly confide in
You had many associates but not real friends
After a while all your bad choices finally caught up to you
Your life hit rock bottom and you didn't know what to do
You stood at a crossroads, one leads to death, the other to life

Through the power of the Holy Spirit you accept the Lord Jesus Christ
At this point you started your exodus from the Egyptian way of life
You were led into the wilderness by the Lord Jesus Christ
In Egypt you used to lie, cheat, and steal to accomplish your tasks
Now you must forsake your former ways, bow your knees and humbly ask
In Egypt you followed the ways of the world in order to meet your needs
Forsake the deeds of the flesh or it is the Holy Spirit whom you will grieve
Out in the wilderness you're being trained how to rely on God
That's why sometimes on the road you walk the way seems so hard
You're no different than Israel as they crossed the burning sand
As they were being led by Christ toward the Promised Land
At Marah the people complained because they had no water to drink
God miraculously made the bitter water sweet enough to drink
God then said, "If you obey all my commands and decrees
I will keep you free from every Egyptian disease"
At the wilderness of Sin they complained because they had nothing to eat
God miraculously provided manna for bread and quail to them for meat
God gave them specific instructions on how to collect this heavenly bread
But they disregarded His commands and did their own thing instead
At Rephidim the people complained, "There's no water to drink!"
Moses said, "Why are you testing the Lord? You better chill out and think!"
They said, "Life was better in Egypt than dying of thirst out here!"
Please don't test the Lord; you must worship Him with reverence and fear

At Mount Sinai God wanted to have a one-on-one relationship with them
But they wanted Moses to speak to God and kept their distance from Him
When Moses went to talk to God and took too long a time
The people forgot all that God had done and committed a spiritual crime
They made a golden calf and offered sacrifices to it
Those who knew better didn't try to make them quit
Because they disregarded the Lord and refused to obey
The Levites killed about 3,000 people that day
When the people refused to go out and conquer the Promised Land
God became angry and made them spend 40 years pounding the sand
God performed miracles in Egypt and the wilderness, but they disregarded His voice
They did not receive what He had promised because they continually made bad choices
All these things happened as an example to you
So that you will know the right things to do
If you don't have water when you desire it
Will this cause you to give up and quit?
When it feels like you're not being fed
Will your hunger cause you to be misled?
When God desires a more intimate relationship with you
Will you draw closer to Him or allow others to do the praying for you?
When God tells you to go out and fight
Will you disobey His word and shake with fright?
When it seems like God is taking too long for you
Will you build a golden calf and commit adultery too?
God knows the beginning from the end
He has predestined that you should win
Stop allowing all the things that are happening around you
To influence you to do what you know you should not do

Every hardship that you will face
Qualifies you for much more grace
If you follow the process and obey His will
His peace will be your strength and the enemy will be still
When you hit a hard place this is what you must do
Remember all the miracles God performed for you
Every time you think, "Well, this is the end!"
God miraculously provides a way for you to win
Just because you are under an attack
Is not a reason for you to go back
No matter what you have to go through
Remember that God is faithful and true
Without faith you cannot stand
Without faith you cannot enter the Promised Land
Egypt is no longer an option for you
Trust in the Lord and do all that He requires of you
DON'T GO BACK!

Motives

Are you using your praise as currency to get things?

We must worship the Father in spirit and in truth
Give praise and thanksgiving; don't stand there like a mute
Worship from a pure heart brings a smile to the Father's face
Praise for selfish motives is a total disgrace
What is it that motivates you to do the things you do?
Is it a sincere love for the Father or what He can do for you?
Are you freely praising the Lord to express your love for Him?
Or are you using your praise as currency to trade with Him?
Is your number one desire to be with the Lord?
If your answers delay will you soon become bored?
Are you more interested in the gift or the Gift giver?
Will you go back to your own agenda once the Lord delivers?
How would you feel if every time your kids came to you?
They had their hands stuck out wanting something from you?
It wouldn't feel good; you would think you're being used
Manipulating your affections, you're being emotionally abused
How dare you think you can manipulate God?
By giving Him praise from an insincere heart
Examine yourself, are your motives true?
Only God and you knows what's on the inside of you
If your worship without is not a reflection of what is within
Then you're trying to manipulate God for your own selfish ends
Emotions are not how you judge if your worship is sincere
True worship is born of love and a reverential fear
Don't be deceived, to yourself be true
Pursue the Father and the blessings will overtake you

Who Could Put a Price Tag on That?

In the spirit your reputation is gained in obscurity
I don't have to wait for any man to acknowledge me
You sacrificed Yourself for me on Calvary
Who could put a price tag on that?

I don't have to anxiously wait for man to give me a chance
I don't have to compromise my values to improve my circumstance
If I place my trust in You my station in life You will advance
Who could put a price tag on that?

I don't have to advertise and sell myself to get the notice of man
I follow the beat of another drummer and not the world's band
My times are in Your hands and You will make me stand
Who could put a price tag on that?

So when life doesn't seem to be all that you think it ought to be
Remember Jesus Christ is your Lord and He is also your Victory
He opens doors no man can close if you walk in loyalty
Who could put a price tag on that?

Time Is the Only Seed You Need

For everything you desire in life
For every resource that you need
Don't get into worry or strife
Time is the only seed you need

Faith without works is dead
God will bless the work of your hands
If you want to reap plenty of bread
You must sow time into the land

Time is your currency on the earth
You can trade it for whatever you need
You demonstrate everything's worth
By how much time you sow as a seed

You show what you really love
By how much time you're willing to invest
Whatever gets most of your time
Is first love because it receives your best

If you're not at the place you want to be
Then listen closely and take heed

Time is the only seed you need

Time Alone

Lord I so enjoy our time alone
Exquisite intimacy shared between us two
My heart overflows with love and joy
As I sing love songs and praises in the night
The nearness of Your Presence surrounds me like a womb
As You nourish and insulate me from the cares of this life
I cannot form the words that adequately describe
The love I feel for You in my inner man
My heart longs for You and the nearness of Your touch
When You touch me I melt on the inside
The decision I made to accept You as Lord I will never ever regret

Seeds, Trees, and Fruit

Even so every good tree bears good fruit; but the bad tree bears bad fruit. A good tree cannot produce bad fruit, nor can a bad tree produce good fruit. Matthew 7:17-18

The only difference between a seed and a full grown tree is its form and what stage it is at in the maturity process. An apple seed is the infantile form of an apple tree. Once a seed is planted and fed it begins the process of becoming what it naturally is. It starts transforming from one form to another. The Word of God is seed. When you first receive that word it is in an infantile state, but as it is fed and watered it starts to grow until it transforms you.

We are in the process of becoming like Christ. The reason the seed matures faster in some people than in others is the way their gardens are tended. Is that seed being watered on a regular basis? Is it receiving enough light? Are the weeds being taken out so the plants aren't choked?

Are you spending time in the light of His Presence? Is that word being watered on a regular basis? Are you abstaining from unproductive activities and carnal foods?

A seed is planted with the purpose of producing something. What seeds are being planted in the ground of your mind? Use discernment. Don't just look at the present time but look down the road. What will those activities, and words, and images, and information that you're being exposed to become when they mature? What kind of a harvest will they produce? Jesus is the Author and the Finisher of our faith. In other words you will know your end if you look at your beginning.

........And let there be trees that grow seed bearing fruit. The seeds will then produce the kinds of plants and trees from which they came. Genesis 1:11

You truly are what you eat.

The fruit of your life is the things that you do
Who you are is revealed by the choices made by you
A tree has no control over the fruit it produces
Jesus said you would know others by their fruit
The process begins by the planting of a seed
The fertile ground of the mind is where it is received
When that seed is first planted it is hidden from sight
The roots go down before it breaks the surface seeking light
The water is the hearing which supplies nourishment to the seed
The better it is fed the faster it does what it was meant to achieve
You are what you are and your fruit is the natural result of that
Apple trees can't produce oranges, that's not a theory just a fact
A seed contains all within it to produce all that it will be
Fleshly seeds put you in bondage, spiritual seeds make you free
The only difference between a seed and a full-grown tree
Is the place in time that each happen to be
The things that I speak, see, read or hear
Are seeds that produce faith or seeds that produce fear
Let's take the mystery out of life and make it as simple as can be
If you use a little discernment this will make you free
There were two trees in the garden; you make the choice where you will eat
You will either walk in light and victory or walk in darkness and defeat
Words are seeds and they are powerful tools
But they get misused when handled by fools
A soft answer turns away anger, wise men know this
A fool hurls insults and tries to solve his problems with his fists
A word of encouragement makes glad a sad heart
But discouraging words can stop you before you even get a good start
Seeds come from the fruit and the fruit comes from the tree

If you trace the information back to its source you can see what the effect on you will be
Words are the seeds and your actions are the fruit
If you want change to occur you must go back to the root
How can you change if you're still planting seeds from the wrong source?
You must start planting new seeds in order to set yourself on a new course

As a Man Thinketh

To go to the next level there are challenges you must face
Obstacles and bumps in the road to keep you from finishing the race
Sometimes you have to come face to face with the things you most fear
Other times you have to let go those things you hold most dear
In other words; there are just some things about you that must change
When you're being tested and your flesh is hurting think it not strange
God will give you the grace you need to pass each and every test
If you stay connected to Him and continually abide in His Rest
The key to appropriating the promises of God lies in the way you think
If you take your eyes off Jesus you'll soon start to sink
Whatever you keep in your eyes and ears your thinking conforms too
An inventory of what gets most of your time will show why you do what you do
These mindsets are given to us at a very early age
The stinking thinking passed on to you keeps you locked in a cage
Jesus came to give us life and that more abundantly
You'll always walk through life with fetters on if your mind isn't free
Renewal of the mind isn't something you bring about by the power of your will
It only comes about with time spent in His Word and as you're Spirit-filled
Where you are right now is the place you need to be
What you learn where you are will help others to be free
Some of the things the Lord removes from you feel like your personality

But the Word is sharp, dividing soul and spirit, shaping you for your destiny
Change is never easy but if you remain persistent and pray
Somewhere in the future you're a better person than you are today

Suffering for Christ's Sake

And indeed all who desire to live godly in Christ Jesus will be persecuted. 2 Timothy 3:12

..."Through many tribulations we must enter the Kingdom of God." Acts 14:22

For to you it has been granted for Christ's sake, not only to believe in Him, but also to suffer for His sake. Philippians 1:29

These things I have spoken to you, that in Me you may have peace. In the world you have tribulation, but take courage; I have overcome the world. John 16:33

Every time you take a stand
When you resist the fear of man
When the world says you can't but the Bible says you can
You're suffering for Christ's sake

When people despitefully use and mistreat you
When people shoot arrows from the dark and lie on you
When you get punished for doing the things you ought to do
You're suffering for Christ's sake

When your spouse cheats on you and you choose to forgive
And every time you think about it it hurts you still
But you're determined to obey God and to do His will
You're suffering for Christ's sake

Instead of compromising you choose to stand alone
When others are out drinking you choose to stay at home
Instead of waking up in strange beds you decide not to roam
You're suffering for Christ's sake

You try to be a blessing to your boss
You want to make them look good at any cost
Then they lie on you and report what's false
You're suffering for Christ's sake

When there's an activity that you love to do
Then the Lord tells you to stop, this is not for you
Your flesh starts to rebel but you still remain true
You're suffering for Christ's sake

When you try to raise your children to do what's right
And they choose to walk in darkness instead of His light
Whenever you talk to them they want to argue, fuss, and fight
You're suffering for Christ's sake

We are called to Re-present Jesus on the Earth
We were given this commission on the day of our rebirth
When you go against the current you know it will hurt
It has been granted to us not only to believe, but also to suffer for Christ's sake

Re-present

Our mission as Christians on the Earth
Is to live a life that demonstrates the miracle of the New Birth
You witness to the lost by the choices you make
The way you live show them if your Christianity is genuine or fake
We never realize how many people are affected by our walk
We must be careful that the way we live lives up to our talk
The closest thing to Jesus most people will see
Is the Light of His Presence reflected through me
While you're at work or you're at play
You interact with the people in your world everyday
You never know who is watching you
To your Lord and Savior you must remain true
People are tired of hypocrisy and the deceitfulness of man
They are looking for a truth on which they can stand
They want more, much more than they're experienced in life
They desire the freedom that only comes through a relationship with Christ
You're the closest thing to Jesus that will ever be seen by them
How you live your life is how the world judges Him
Are you living your life in such a way that His Light is reflected through you?
Can people tell where your affinities lie by the choices made by you?
Are you the same person no matter whose company you're in?
Or do you act holier than thou with the saints and with sinners wallow in sin?
Do you forgive when mistreated? Do you pray for those who despitefully use you?
Do you go out of your way to help the needy?
When tempted do you remain faithful and true?
We are called to be His witnesses, but not just by the words that we say
By your acts of kindness, do you show the world, our Lord and His Way?

When you're around the saints you're on your best behavior
When family or friends treat you unfairly do you still show them favor?
How can you forgive if you've never been wronged?
If you refuse to forgive how can people ever atone?
How can you love your enemy if one doesn't exist?
The impulse for vengeance is what you must resist
How can you demonstrate the nature of Christ?
Without exposing yourself to pain in this life
How will you know God and His Way?
If a wall separates you from the world everyday
How can God be your Healer if you're never ill?
You'll never know Him in that way if you're out of His Will
How can God be a Strong Tower if you neglect your responsibility?
You will only know Him in this way as you engage the enemy
How can God be your Provider if you're never in need?
You'll never know Him in this way if you're susceptible to greed
We can live an overcoming life in these last days
Only if we acknowledge Him in all our ways
Fulfill the purpose God placed within you
The time for talk is over; it's now time to do

Honor God in All you Do

God inhabits His people's praise
Magnify His Name all of your days
In spite of the trouble facing you
Honor the Lord in all you do
As you attempt to take new ground
Know that the enemy will be around
As the enemy tries to overwhelm you
Honor the Lord in all you do
Whoever reality you chose to believe
Is whose objectives are being achieved
The enemy wants you to see sin and defeat
He only wants to kill, steal and cheat
Cheat you of the blessings God promised to you
By believing the lie he presents to you
But the Word of God is a rock upon which you can stand
It's time to stop crying like a baby and start acting like a man
The Word of God is more real than those things you can see
The Word of God is the ultimate reality
The trial you now face is light affliction indeed
To overcome your spirit man you must start to feed

Fulfill Your Duty

Your present circumstances are ordained by God
Don't be fearful or anxious on the road you now trod
God lets the rain falls on the just and unjust too
To be more like God this is what you must also do
What is my purpose for being here on the Earth?
Why didn't I die on the day of my birth?
How did I survive all those years without knowing him?
I seek understanding because my light is dim
There's no such thing as luck in the life of a saint
Sometimes your trials are so bad you just want to faint
But if I'm self-centered only thinking about me
I will never fulfill my God ordained destiny
Your life is not your own it belongs to the Lord
You gave up your right to choose when He severed sin's cord
Your goal is not to live a comfortable life
It's to live in submission to the Lord Jesus Christ
Whatever trouble or circumstances the Lord leads you to
Will work together for your good if you do what He tells you to do
That person who angrily gets in your face
Is an opportunity for you to dispense grace
The person who cut you off on your way to work
Is a soul in need of intercession not some conceited jerk
The boss who rides your back day after day
Doesn't need criticism, they need you to pray
You were sent out to be a light in a dark place
When you attempt to take new ground new enemies you'll face
This warfare isn't fought against physical things
Spiritual warfare is fought against unseen beings
People are the vessels they use to express their desires
The offense of man has caused many saints to retire
They fought a fleshly warfare against an ignorant slave
Instead of spiritual battle against spirits who are depraved
You are not a baby so God didn't give you a rattle
You are a Spirit-filled Saint being trained for battle

You must direct your warfare against the enemy
If you want to see your loved ones escape captivity
You will engage the enemy so be ready to fight
Victory only comes as you walk in the Light

Bless and Never Curse

And I will bless those who bless you, and the one who curses you I will curse.
Genesis 12:3

Many Christians aren't prospering and moving forward because they haven't discerned the Body of Christ. When you pronounce a curse against another Christian the promise of Genesis 12:3 comes into play. This promise applies to all the descendants of Abraham. When you speak evil of one another a curse is placed on you. The most common place for this is in the home. Husbands and wives who speak evil toward one another do so because they haven't discerned the Body of Christ. Whatever you say or do to your spouse you are in reality doing to yourself because you are one flesh. When you mistreat and speak evil to your spouse you are committing the equivalent of spiritual self-mutilation. It's no wonder you can't get ahead, you are your own worst enemy. The devil has deceived you. He has tricked you into using the power and authority given to you by God against yourself. Because you lack spiritual discernment you fail to realize how the words of your mouth harm you. The Bible describes words in many ways. They are swords, arrows, darts, and clubs. I pray that every time you speak in an ungodly manner you will see in the spirit the effect your words have on the person you're talking to or talking about just as if you were using a physical weapon against them.

Suicide in the natural is a horrible tragedy
Depression and anger blind the eyes to the real enemy
Someone taking their own life is something we don't condone
You try to convince them life's worth living when they call you on the phone
The act of killing another person is a very extreme case
But it happens every day, and it's something we must face
The taking of life is not tolerated in the natural

But millions are killed every day in the spiritual
God gave you the power to speak death or life
When you curse with your mouth you pay a very high price
Spiritual suicide and homicide is a terrible tragedy
With their mouths people place themselves into captivity
When God says "All things are possible" and you say it can't be done
You've turned your weapons upon yourself and the enemy has won
If someone had a gun to their temple and said, "I'm blowing myself away
You would cry, plead, call the police, get on your knees and pray
But when someone speaks evil about themselves we don't give it a second thought
You can't see the wounds being inflicted, because you're unlearned and untaught
Every day in the world people are being killed in the streets
The violence is everywhere, there's no place to retreat
People dying senseless deaths because others don't value life
Lack of morals in our country carries a very high price
But right at school, home, work, or play
People are murdered before our eyes everyday
Children too young to defend themselves are marked and cursed for life
Many stay in that condition until they come to know Jesus Christ
People who are weak without a sense of identity
Are like spiritual chameleons, always changing, into what people say they should be
If you're in a position of authority you must know this
A rebuke from you to a subordinate is more painful than a boxer's fist
How many youth have lost their purpose because of the words some teacher said?
They grow up never fulfilling their destiny because they ate the words they were fed
Adults oppressed by fear and still afraid of the dark

Are the children who had words spoken to them that placed their life in park?
I must be responsible for what I say, discipline starts with me
You say what you say because the consequences are so hard to see
You have no knowledge that the things you say are a spiritual force
The words we speak accepted by the hearer can set their life course
Bless and never curse, for this is the only way
Or the evil that you speak will come upon you one day

God is Calling You to Nineveh

When God called Jonah to preach to Nineveh
The prophet became outraged and went into fits
God loves all people and this city He wanted to save
Even though its inhabitants were wholly evil and depraved
Nineveh was the enemy of Israel
They conquered God's people and the nation fell
They were known far and wide for their cruelty
They ruthlessly attacked others and placed them in captivity
God saw their evil acts and judgment was ready to fall
To save this evil city was the reason Jonah received the call
Jonah was a man like many of us
He knew God was faithful and His Word he could trust
Israel was the recipient of many of Nineveh's evil acts
Jonah didn't want them spared he wanted God to attack
Jonah chose to run from the Presence of God
As a result of his choice he had a hard road to trod
His disobedience brought grief into the lives of others
Don't let your sin bring evil consequences into the life of another
Who are the people in your life?
Who oppress you like the Ninevites?
People who add bitterness to your life
As you try to live for Jesus Christ
People who you are waiting for God to judge
People you won't pray for because you hold a grudge
The evil people in your life
Are no different than the Ninevites
When you were deep in your sin God still loved you
Loving the evil people in your life is what God requires of you
When you refuse to humble yourself, intercede and pray
You are no different than Jonah who ran away
Your disobedience will come with a very high cost
If you refuse to pray for an evil boss
If you refuse to do what you know is right
You may end up in a place devoid of light

At the end of the day God will accomplish this task
So why not just do what the Lord has asked?
God loves these evil people just like He loves you
Submit yourself to the Lord do what he asks you to do

It's Your Duty to Pray

"But I say to you, love your enemies, and pray for those who persecute you in order that you may be sons of your Father who is in heaven; for He causes His sun to rise on the evil and the good, and sends rains on the righteous and the unrighteous. For if you love those who love you, what reward have you? Do not even the tax-gathers do the same? And if you greet your brothers only, what do you do more than others? Do not even the Gentile do the same? Therefore you are to be perfect, as your heavenly Father is perfect. Matthew 5:44-48

"But love your enemies, and do good, and lend, expecting nothing in return, and your reward will be great, and you will be sons of the Most High; for He Himself is kind to ungrateful and evil men. Luke 6:35

I urge you therefore brethren, by the mercies of God, to present your bodies a living and holy sacrifice, acceptable to God, which is your spiritual service of worship.
Roman 12:1

The time for procrastinating is way over due
The age of selfish Christianity should be over too
It's time to stop focusing on our needs and the things that we face
To rediscover our purpose and get back in the race
If the flea ruled over the lion we would ask ourselves why?
Christian submitted to the world should bring a tear to your eye
The Lord's body on the earth allows the world to be its master
We don't exercise our authority and the world is on the brink of disaster
People going to hell because there's no one to intercede
Not many Christians are willing to minister to the gentile's needs
Not many willing to sacrifice to save the lost
Not many willing to sacrifice and pay the cost

We're willing to send others to make disciples in foreign lands
But in the place where the Lord placed us we're unwilling to take a stand
Your checkbook will tell the values you have in this life
How you spend your time shows if you're a disciple of Jesus Christ
Does it bother you to see the people that you work with every day?
Will spend an eternity in hell if you don't witness and pray
Don't you realize that you're in an army and that we are at war?
It's time to stop thinking about your own needs and start doing your chores
A soldier doesn't concern himself in the affairs of this life
He's focused on the mission he received from the Lord Jesus Christ
You think the only reason you got that job is to feed your family?
No! The Lord placed you there so those people could be free
Because you don't have an understanding you're wasting a lot of time
Disobeying orders in the military is considered a crime
You don't have to be pushy and get all in people's way
You just have to make a commitment to pray for them everyday
Every revival came as the result of the prayers of diligent men
You staying in place, on your face, is part of God's plan
If not you then who? If not now then when?
They're under your care and it's your responsibility to defend
Those people have no idea that there's a fight over their soul
You must be faithful, determined, persistent, diligent and bold
When you go through various trials and tests all eyes are on you
How you weather the storm will be their first clue
As you continue to stand through floods that sweep others away
A seed will be sown in their mind and they will approach you someday
They know you have something that they do not possess
When their heart is open then you can begin to confess
You tell them that Jesus is how you made it through

You tell them He did this for me and He will also do it for you
Not in excellency of speech, but in the Spirit and with power
Now is the time! Now is the hour!

Love Starts at Home

Love is patient and kind. Love is not jealous or boastful or proud or rude. It does not demand its own way. It is not irritable, and it keeps no record of being wronged. It does not rejoice about injustice but rejoices whenever the truth wins out. Love never gives up, never loses faith, is always hopeful and endures through every circumstance.
1st Corinthians 13:4-7

Our purpose is noble, our mission is clear
To spread the love of God to those held in bondage to fear
Our purpose is the reach the seekers and lost
To accomplish that task we will spare no cost
So we make church seeker friendly and play music that pleases
In the hope that someone will find Jesus and fall to their knees
That is our purpose; it's the reason we're here
Sometimes we're so focused on loving strangers we neglect those we hold dear
To fulfill the Great Commission to the ends of the Earth we will roam
But so often we forget that love starts at home
We come to church with smiles painted on our faces
Hypocritically playing our parts and going through the paces
We are so consumed with how people at church view us
We hold our tempers in check and we dare not cuss
But at home we are different; at home we can be free
Your family knows very well all your inconsistencies
At home we're impatient, rude and demand our own way
The different between when you're at home and church is like night and day
You've become a stumbling block to your children by the things that you do
They think church is a joke and all Christians are hypocritical like you
Like a chameleon at church your true colors you hide

But those closest to you see through all your lies
You want to spread the love of Christ and to the ends of the Earth you will roam
My friend, don't forget this truth, love starts at home
You're a leader in ministry and your focus is on Christ
In a world full of darkness you want to be a light
When you speak to the lost you carefully choose your words
First impressions are important, or so you've heard
You would never, ever speak to a seeker in a disrespectful tone
But you say whatever you feel to those at home
Home in this instance is the ministry you lead
And those who serve under you would be your family
In the interests of running a well oiled ministry you often speak out of turn
And what you say to those who serve with you oftentimes burns
You're so focused on how your ministry appears to those on the outside
But you're so condescending and disrespectful to those who serve by your side
By your words and actions you make those who serve with you feel all alone
WAKE-UP CALL! Remember true love starts at home
Being a leader in any organization is a very hard task
Being a leader in the Church is almost more than anyone can ask
As a leader what's good about the organization is a reflection of the good in you
But what's wrong with the organization is also a reflection of you
When you look at the church the changes are obvious to see
What's not so obvious is the fact that change in the church starts with me
It's easy to excuse your own sin and point your finger at others
But remove the log from your eye before attempting to remove the speck from your brother's
The most loving thing that a leader can do
Is to be what he desires to see in you
You teach what you know, but reproduce what you are

If you neglect what's in your own heart the church won't go very far
As a leader you are tasked to maintain order
You must keep ministry leaders on the right side of the border
Failing to correct someone subordinate to you
Lessens the effectiveness of all you attempt to do
When correction is given it doesn't feel good at all
But a timely rebuke can prevent a future downfall
Turning a blind eye to issues that should be faced
Sends a double message to people, and leads to disgrace
What's in your heart to abundance is reflected in your life
If the light within you is darkness, you cannot reflect the light of Christ
Failing to deal with the darkness guarantees you will not win
Often a timely correction is not given because you're too careful not to offend
Man of God; Serve with courage and integrity and don't give in to fear
A loving leader corrects those who they hold dear
In an effort to win the lost to the ends of the Earth we will roam
Don't forget, true love starts in your heart, and is demonstrated to those at home

Submission

Submitting to authority is for your protection
You expose yourself to danger when you refuse correction
A little disobedience may seem okay
But that one little act could ruin your day
A lifetime of good works gone in the blink of an eye
Because you rebelled against authority your future's gone bye-bye
Your parents tried to lead you in the right way
They tried to pass on their wisdom to you every day
But their words went in one ear and out the other
As they talked you zoned out on your father and mother
Every time they tried to warn you in the past
What they said would happen happened, it always came to pass
Something within you wouldn't allow you to submit to their authority
Their rules were too confining, you wanted to be free
All your classmates and friends get to do whatever they want to do
You feel like you're missing all the fun, you want to party too
The only thing you're missing is a whole lot of pain
There's no such thing as love at 16, these boys are playing games
To get what they want anything they will say
To get you to do things their own way
They will make all kinds of promises to you
Once they get what they want then they're through
All they are looking for is sex
If you give in you'll soon be their "Ex"

Submission is your Mission

It is man's responsibility to keep the family on track
He is supposed to guard the gate and keep the enemy back
You can trace most of the problems in society
To men who act irresponsibly
Absentee fathers who selfishly leave their families so they can roam
Cause their children to grow up without a strong male role model at home
Adulterous husbands who go out and cheat on their wives
Cause unimaginable heartbreak and bring bitterness into their lives
Men of the flesh who squander all their money on drugs and drinks
Create instability in their families and cause them to slowly sink
Disloyal sons who rebel against their parents to go their own way
Break their parent's heart and will reap a harvest of bitterness someday
The violent man with an uncontrollable temper who physically abuses his wife
Dwells in deep darkness and is no longer following the Lord Jesus Christ
Healthy men are the key to having healthy families
A man fully submitted to Jesus always walks in victory
Jesus the firstborn of many sons paid an awfully high price
God's desire is that every man become like Jesus Christ
A man fully submitted to God will obey His two great commands
To love the Lord with all your heart, and also love your fellow man
A man fully submitted to Jesus will not mistreat his wife
He will raise godly children and live an overcoming life
A man fully submitted to Jesus everyday choices are God's will
This man is led by the Spirit and not by how he feels
A man fully submitted to Christ humbles himself and prays
He's in constant intercession for his family all throughout the day
A man fully submitted to God is an example at his work

He does his job without supervision, and his duties he will not shirk
The key to changing society
Is for men to act responsibly
To bring society out of darkness and into His Light
We need more men fully submitted to the Lord Jesus Christ

The Crucified Life

Being a chameleon will never do
You must worship the Lord in Spirit and in Truth
If you change how you look based on the environment you're in
When you face off against the enemy how can you ever hope to win?
The people closest to you see your inconsistencies
And deep down in your heart you're longing to be free
At church you're all smiles and you keep your temper in check
But at home you're a raging lunatic and your home is a wreck
At church you lift your hands and say "Amen!"
At home you say words that shouldn't be repeated again
At church you're the first one to put money in the plate
But when your children have a need you tell them they have to wait
At church you give hugs and pats on the back
At home your family is the recipient of your verbal attacks
At church you volunteer for all kinds of tasks
At home you won't do anything that your wife asks
At church you give the appearance that you hold your family dear
But the reality is that your family lives in a constant state of fear
It's time to stop all the hypocrisy
Your life needs more consistency
It's time to grow deeper into Jesus Christ
It's time for you to live the crucified life
Anything within you that doesn't look like the Lord
Is something that you can no longer afford
The time for pretense is way over due
Honesty is the way to receive your breakthrough
Who you are isn't reflected by your behavior with your brothers
But in the choices you make out in the world when you interact with others
If the people in your world can't see the Jesus in you
It's an indication that you have more work to do
It's time for you to stop excusing sin

It's time for you to forsake all and enter in
Your home is full of anger, division, and strife
Because you refuse to bear your cross and live a crucified life
You release words into the atmosphere
That curse the very ones that you hold dear
Life and death are in the power of the tongue
Those who love it will eat its fruit
If you want a life that pleases God
Stop flailing at branches and put the axe to the root
It's time to be brutally honest with yourself
It's time to put your excuses on the shelf
It's time to fully commit to Jesus Christ
It's time to bear your cross and live a crucified life
It's time to repent to your family
When you decide to change you can help them to be free
If you want to be pleasing in God's sight
You must start living the crucified life

The Lighthouse

A lighthouse sits on a craggy rock all alone
Its sole purpose in life is to guide wayward ships home
Many lives have been saved because the lighthouse faithfully showed it light
Helping many vessels lost at sea maneuver through the night
Not many thank the light man for faithfully carrying out his tasks
He faithfully discharged his duties without being asked
Many of you are the only light the world can see
Standing firm for the cause of Christ can be quite lonely
Faithfully doing His Will in both sun and rain
When times are good, when times are bad, when you have nothing to gain
Doing good to those who show no gratitude to you
Can tempt you to stop doing the things you ought to do
Rain or shine, calm or storm the lighthouse shines its light
Leading and guiding those who struggle to maneuver through the night
You are a bearer of Christ's light
He trusted you to do what's right
To re-present Him on the Earth
To put yourself second and put others first
Obey the calling on your life
Be a light to others who struggle at night
Let His Light be reflected in you
By the choices you make and the things that you do
In your world be the lighthouse that brightly shines your light
Leading those who are lost to the Lord Jesus Christ

Maturity Is Security

A child in the kingdom is no better than a slave
Because his mind is not renewed even though the price been paid
He is heir of all his Daddy owns
But he can't get his inheritance until he has grown
Christians are perishing because they just don't know
They think that people are their problem but to the Spirit they must go
You must wrestle, but not with flesh and blood
Your fight is in the Spirit with principalities up above
Fussing and fighting with each other isn't wise
You think that person is your problem but it's the devil in disguise
A mature person will forgive and turn his back on strife
A child takes the bait and lets the devil steal his light
A child is selfish; he only wants to get his way
A child speaks and acts before he goes off to pray
Seeking for position to build his self-esteem
He won't submit to authority and become part of the team
It's time to grow up and stop playing games
It's time to admit your faults and stop seeking to place blame
It's time to be responsible and own up to your mistakes
It's time to become a blessing and stop being a big headache

www.ingramcontent.com/pod-product-compliance
Ingram Content Group UK Ltd.
Pitfield, Milton Keynes, MK11 3LW, UK
UKHW041939190726
13854UKWH00004B/1691